Aberdeens
around the
World

From the ancient castles,

pine forests

and wooded
valleys of
Aberdeenshire,
Scotland

. . . to prairie skies,

High Sierra

and tropical jungle

Aberdeens around the World

Strandloopers, Turpentine and Little Green Ants

Recollections of a Global Journey

Frederick Bull

Scottish Cultural Press
www.scottishbooks.com

Dedicated to my brother, Tom

To Margaret, Stuart and Lindsay for knowing why,
and to all who assisted.
Thank you.

First published 2004 by
SCOTTISH CULTURAL PRESS
Unit 6, Newbattle Abbey Business Park
Newbattle Road, Dalkeith, EH22 3LJ, Scotland
Tel: +44 (0)131 660 6366 • Fax: +44 (0)131 660 4666
Email: info@scottishbooks.com
www.scottishbooks.com

Front cover main illustration of Union Street, Aberdeen, reproduced by
kind permission of Aberdeen and Grampian Tourist Board, Scotland,
all others copyright © Frederick Bull and Alan White

BRITISH LIBRARY CATALOGUING IN PUBLICATION DATA
A catalogue record for this book is available from the British Library

ISBN: 1 84017 045 X

Printed and bound by ColourBooks Ltd, Dublin

CONTENTS

A Hilltop, Pine Barrens and Cotton Fields

Desert, Beach and an Island Paradise

Thorn Bush, Eucalyptus and Bamboo

The amount of townships around the world which flourish under the proud name of Aberdeen is a fair indication of the numbers as well as the calibre of people who left these Scottish shores to make their mark in foreign parts.

Perhaps unaware of it until they had arrived, those exiles had taken with them a background of sound education and ethical standards which would not only give a head start in their chosen careers but would equip them for leadership as well.

Such were the expectations back home, I have long believed that, if you can do it in the North East of Scotland, you can do it even better elsewhere. So Aberdonians have made their mark wherever they have gone – and not a few have transplanted the name of that beloved city twixt Dee and Don which would be forever in their blood. It has long been a proud boast that there is a whole host of Aberdeens out there in the big wide world. Americans could always rattle off a good selection of their own. What is perhaps surprising, in an age when very little is left unexplored, is that nobody had bothered to bring forth the evidence under one cover.

While not claiming a completely exhaustive collection (always slightly hazardous when some 'helpful person' is liable to produce an omission from Outer Mongolia), nevertheless, Frederick Bull gives us an impressive list of communities, almost all of which he has visited, and which share a name with the mother hen of all Aberdeens.

They run down from North America from Nova Scotia and Saskatchewan through the Marylands and Carolinas and across to Washington State and south to California. Halfway across, you drive into Aberdeen, South Dakota, and find that Frank Baum lived there, he who wrote *The Wonderful Wizard of Oz*.

The discoveries stretch onwards to Jamaica, Antigua, South Africa, an island in the Indian Ocean, Australia and, of course, Hong Kong, where the harbour area twinkles like a large-scale 'Fittie'.

Frederick Bull sets the scene with his own evocative description of the original Aberdeen, intertwining a potted history with rich memories of his own childhood in the city, dating from the war.

He began his research from the distance of Ayrshire, where he has been a college lecturer in Art and Design.

But he does so in retirement, which has taken him back to his native heath with all the vigour of a returning exile.

This well illustrated volume will flesh out those vague assertions that the world is full of Aberdeens.

Jack Webster
Journalist and Author

INTRODUCTION

Scots have been seafaring people for many centuries, settling in all corners of the world and contributing to the growth of new townships in distant countries. For many, their sense of exile was eased by sharing the name of their birthplace with their new community.

Scots place names can be found on all the continents, and the name 'Aberdeen' can be seen on maps from the coasts and prairies of Canada and America, to the islands of the Caribbean, South America and Africa; from the Bay of Bengal to ancient China and a valley in Australia.

Some years ago, I heard of a small handful of cities and townships called 'Aberdeen' and became curious as to how many more locations world-wide might share the name of my home. Documents, road maps, atlases and publications unearthed in libraries provided what I needed, and I began to compile a list of names and addresses which would later prove to be valuable sources in my 'detective work'. This led to global correspondence and within weeks the initial slow trickle of response became a deluge as replies flooded back from enthusiastic contacts in other Aberdeens. Local post offices, historical societies, newspaper editors, journalists, mayors, town councils, tourism departments, heritage centres and local citizens began telling me of their communities. Each shared my enthusiasm for our collective discovery.

Some correspondents sent published material containing comprehensive details of the history and development of their towns. Others researched on my behalf. In Jamaica, a photographer and journalist travelled two hundred kilometres to collect information about the Aberdeen near Black River. In New South Wales, Australia, a determined lady set about compiling the previously fragmented history of her town. These new friends have as much ownership of this research as myself.

At the end of almost eight years, I was confident that all of the Aberdeens had been revealed. The excitement of discovering more than thirty drove me towards the next obvious quest. They had to be visited!

This apparently unachievable ambition occupied my energies for the next two years. However, I realised that, if my desire to visit these Aberdeens was to have any meaning, it had to be an experience which could be shared. The answer was to film my journey and produce a video so that others could see these places and hear from local people.

Now that the target was in focus, I waited for the lucky break! We all know that effort and good fortune can make dreams come true. Could I be that lucky?

Lady Fortune did favour me and, ten years after beginning the research, I met up with Alan White, a film-maker and fellow Aberdonian. He shared my excitement at the prospect of filming the Aberdeens around the world. With the support of Aberdeen City Council and many other enthusiasts of the project, the funding was raised and preparation for the long, ninety-five thousand mile journey around the world began.

What an adventure it became. All thoughts of fatigue evaporated in anticipation of meeting up with my correspondents and many new friends. And visiting the Aberdeens, of course!

The global trek was more fulfilling than I could ever have imagined; the warmth of welcome in each community exceeded all expectations and during my travels I became aware of a 'family of Aberdeens' around the world, each member keen to know of the others and enthusiastic about our shared heritage.

On return to Scotland there was the task of editing hours of film footage. The resulting video, *In Search of Aberdeen*, has given me a magic carpet which transports me back to each community. Watching it, I am able to return to some of the fine people and wonderful locations which I had the good fortune to visit.

I learned something of their history – the early years of struggle and determination, major local historical events and the efforts of people to conserve their past. However, wondrous as the journey most certainly was and delightful as the images are in the video, there is so much more to learn of the Aberdeens. There are communities which have grown, others which have all but vanished. Each has as much passion about its identity, and place in history, as we have here in Scotland.

Curiosity led me to this project and it is shared. Each Aberdeen discovered has become a link in a global chain. There is quiet pride in my Scottish roots, as I realise that my fellow countrymen have spread so far

From Aberdeen, Scotland, to many others

across the planet from our small country. Our forebears were truly remarkable.

One request which persisted made me carry out my own local research. 'Tell me about Aberdeen, Scotland.'

Not the easiest of tasks! There are others who have eloquently told the story of Aberdeen's history, growth and development. Understandably, I baulked at the thought of tackling such a major task and it is with some trepidation that I attempt a summary of the city's long story. In common with the other great cities of Scotland, it is a story of dramatic change, defiant struggle and survival. But, to most Aberdonians, the place means so much more than that. It is the environment in which we were forged, polished and sent forth. As with all communities in which we pass our younger years, we are products of the culture, people, places and events which entered our lives. Reflection on some of these 'growing up' experiences may reveal more of the city, its ways, and why I hold it so dear. My childhood recollections will be shared by most north-east folk.

What of the other Aberdeens around the world? Each has a story to tell of people and their times, and of pride in those who put down roots. This I grew to learn and understand as I travelled the world. Repeatedly, I heard of connections with Scotland, in particular to this north-east corner from where so many left.

There are special people out there; it was a privilege to be among them.

Frederick Bull
Logie Coldstone, Aberdeenshire

Fisher-folks cottages at 'Fittie'

The 'Inversnecky' on the Beach Promenade

REFLECTIONS

Even in childhood years we Aberdonians were aware of the vast world beyond the north-east, since most families had at least one relative living abroad. Aberdeen is a major port and, as youngsters, we saw vessels coming into harbour from Poland, Canada, Sweden and other distant countries. There was a constant supply of tales from seafaring folk, but none more amazing than those of my grandfather Alexander Forbes.

'Old Alick' enthralled my brother Tom and I with his exaggerated tales of fishing from the Baltic to the Baffin Islands. He came from a long line of harbour pilots and fishermen well schooled in the art of incredible 'tales of the ocean' and he had a quite romantic relationship with the sea.

'She has to be treated like a woman; treated properly,' he used to say. 'Turn your back, lose interest or respect for her and she will turn on you with wrathful vengeance.'

Alick was a deep-sea fisherman from Footdee or, as we say, 'Fittie', Aberdeen. In that old fishing village at the harbour entrance they like to know who you are, and I can recall early confirmation of my identity. At a family weekend, my genealogy was verified by reference to me as, 'Jessie's, Alickie's, Gwennie's, Freddie'. Those four generations established my lineage beyond reasonable doubt.

Family and neighbours filled me with awe as they yarned of whaling trips to the South Atlantic, or told tales of people or places beyond a young imagination. The world far from the city seemed vast, tempting and full of adventure. They instilled in me a 'wanderlust', a nagging restlessness fairly common to all who live in sea-faring communities. It is an itch which does not go away and, for some, this was to have a powerful impact in later life.

We children learned other values from the farming folk, so steady and reliable in their land-locked stability. We came to understand the challenge that lay in the soil, and the permanence of the landscape.

'Benachie will aye be there, laddie,' an Aberdeenshire farmer reassured.

His words echo from glorious summers spent at the villages of Rhynie,

Oyne and Methlick, as 'Mither Tap' (the highest top on Benachie) kept a keen and watchful eye on her territory.

The city itself was an 'Aladdin's cave' for us energetic youngsters. Tramcars rattled eastwards to the sands of the Sea Beach and westwards to the woodlands of Hazlehead Park. The beach was near my grandparents, Sarah and Alick, who always had pennies for ice-cream from the Washington or the Inversnecky. They are still the two best ice-cream cafes on the promenade.

Punch and Judy shows, donkey rides, sing-songs, sandcastle competitions and the novelty of a tide which playfully flung the cold sea against my wee white legs and ankles made a trip to the beach very special. A salty tide-mark on shoes was all the proof parents needed to know where you had been!

Going to Hazlehead Park was a journey with its own magic. The tramcar left the city and swayed along a tree-lined road into the countryside. There were trees as tall as church spires, some with strange, soft bark; acres of grass on which to run and run; the stage and bandstand for showing off; and the perplexing mysteries of the Maze. Finding the centre was one thing, finding your way out another!

In the heart of the city we explored the New Market and the shops of

Tram cars rattling along King Street in the 1950s

Heading out past Footdee

Open vista of Cromar Valley, Aberdeenshire

Aberdeen City's
Town House

Historic
St Machar
Cathedral

George Street and Union Street. We walked and slithered around the Fish Market, or visited the Harbour to wonder at the vast stacks of sawn timber brought from Sweden and Canada. This was usually followed by a visit to the Joint Station – all noise, bustle and the smell of escaping steam, hot oil and acrid, burning coal. Close to the destination board was a slot machine, which dispensed bars of Five Boys chocolate, and another contraption from which you could stamp out your name on a strip of soft metal.

Such advanced technology. Where would it all end?

Enticing lanes or closes with unusual names connected the larger streets. Drum's Lane, Adelphi Lane, Shoe Lane, Theatre Lane and Peacock's Close were regularly awakened as we shrieked and scampered beneath the large granite buildings which hid these secret places.

The city was our 'activity centre'. Visits to its centre meant taking the tramcar from Woodside Fountain, the conductor magically conjuring tickets from a machine filled with a narrow paper roll. 1940s technology at its very best!

When older, I cycled into town where Maberly Street, partly paved with wooden blocks instead of the usual granite 'cassies', was a great attraction. The smooth silent glide on the wooden surface was for dry days – it was far too slippery in the wet!

Loch Street Co-operative, the Rubber Shop, Windmill Brae, Union Terrace Gardens, the Green, the Broad Hill, the Duthie Park, and more than a dozen cinemas all drew us downtown. Nearer to home was the fascination of the Kittybrewster cattle auctions and the greater temptation of forbidden places like the Dancing Cairns Quarry or the river Don at Grandholm. Climbing back up the many steps of Jacob's Ladder from the Don was our 'fitness regime'. To parents, however, we were always playing at the Stewart Park. The deceit of adventurous youth!

In late autumn, the 'shows' came to town and then the Central Park became a magnet for youngsters. Usually, I went there with Tom or our friends, Edward and Isobel. Such excitement was for sharing. Hardly an evening was missed as we savoured the sound, light, movement and strange electrical smell of it all.

Shows of a different kind were organised in the street by my close friend, Isobel. We borrowed clothes from our parents, dressed up and offered our 'music hall' of song and dance acts. Tickets and posters were made from old school jotters, and Isobel's garden shed was magically transformed into a theatre. We had a glorious time as families came to watch and take part in our afternoon matinees.

Not even the long, dark winter days could diminish our energies. The season was welcomed with the expectation of snow and 1947 and 1948 delivered in abundance. On those wonderful winter evenings we slid and sledged on sugar-crusted snow, marvelling at the star-filled sky, the fiery red ring burning ever more painfully on our legs where wellington boot met flesh. Those gas-lit nights usually ended with a bag of 'tattie fritters' from Lawrence's Chipper held tightly in both hands to restore frozen little fingers. The bitter vinegar was supped from the empty paper bag as a symbol of boyhood courage. Life was as good as it gets!

Learning was firmly delivered at Woodside School, enhanced by my father's teaching during our Sunday Walk. Education did not stop at the school gates! These long Sabbath strolls took place when my father, Jim, was not playing his trombone in the bandstand at either Hazlehead Park or the Duthie Park. As we walked, each street name and its origin, each fine granite building and its purpose was explained. Dad used statues as teaching aids and lessons were often conducted at the feet of Robert Burns or William Wallace! Unknown to us, Tom and I were being imbued with respect for the history of the city. Slowly, we were growing aware of our culture and the contribution made by earlier generations of Scots.

At home, fresh fish from grandfather's 'fry' was prepared so delicately that the skin peeled back at the touch of a fork. Subtly but surely, the eating habits of Aberdeen were being laid down for life through the skills of our very attentive mother, Gwen. My young appetite dealt eagerly with mutton broth, rowies, softies, mince, tatties and skirlie. But my favourite was 'potted heid and stovies' with crumbled oatcake on top. Yum!

The extended business of teenage education was dealt with by homework-laden years at Aberdeen Grammar School, which, incredibly, dates back to 1256 and was attended by Lord Byron in 1795. And later, years of hard work and delight at Gray's School of Art gave me lifelong friends and a professional qualification which led me to teaching Visual Art.

Had Aberdeen finished with me yet?

Not quite. There was the small matter of acquiring fluency in north-east humour. In this city of two lively universities and well-established trades and industries, everyone was an amateur philosopher, exchanging wit with a purpose.

'Time is a device,' a stranger informed me in a city bar. 'It stops a'thing fae happenin' a' at once.' Translation: 'It prevents everything from happening at the same time'. Humorous and profound, the exchange was shared with mutual delight. Throughout the north-east there is still pleasure in the use of challenging wit. Out on the Aberdeenshire hills I once asked a local how far it was to our destination and, quick as a rapier, came the reply.

'Two miles if you walk quick, nearer four miles if you walk slow.'

We all laughed.

Our local dialect has many idiosyncrasies, too. Here, a boy is called a 'loon', a girl a 'quine'. A young boy is a 'loonie', an infant boy a 'loonikie'. This use of the diminutive or familiar is common at the end of nouns. We call it 'couthie spikkin'.

'Want a biscuit*ie*, wi' yer cupp*ie* tea?'

Another favourite is the rather strange use of self-questioning declarations.

'Fine day, is it?' or 'He's big, is he?' or 'They're heavy, are they?'

And the still amusing childhood recollection of buying lemonade.

'A bottle of lemonade, please.'

'Aye, what kind do you want, orange or pineapple?'

The speech of the north-east has absorbed the Doric, an old dialect or remnants of a language, still common among fishing and farming people. We hear it when we come together in our village. Any excuse will do for a ceilidh! Fiddles and accordions sing out, local folks exchange gossip and we laugh tolerantly at the same old jokes. We listen to the old bothy ballads sung in the Doric; our native tongue kept alive in songs like 'My pair o' nicky tams' and 'It's cauld at nicht in the bothy'.

How many times were they sung, in Alberta, West Virginia and beyond? All who left the north-east took with them our language, sentiment and customs. They also took a philosophy to help cope with unexpected change. What better way to deal with Destiny than to shrug one's shoulders and say with typical north-east resignation, 'There's aye a something'. For all Scots who settled in distant lands there was 'aye a something', be it flood, drought, storm, or even worse the impact of war.

This often-used phrase originates in the work of the north-east poet Charles Murray, who sums up the philosophical acceptance that not everything is as it should be, or as we want it to be. Like so many scots,

Murray (born in Alford, rural Aberdeenshire, 1864) spent much of his life abroad. Yet even during his busy years as Secretary for Public Works in South Africa, he found time to write in his native dialect. His poems reflect the droll wit and solemn nonchalance of north-east folks. His poem, 'There's Aye a Something', is a witty comment on an apparently badly matched couple and was written more than a century ago. Little did he know that its humour would become part of north-east culture, and its moral provide a response to all circumstances. As you will read later, to translate Murray's poem from the Doric would be a grave misjudgement.

From early years, amusement and delight in language have been embedded in my generation. Has all of this changed?

Yes, the city has changed. The fishing industry has been overtaken by the oil industry and the pace of life appears to be less contemplative. However, the dry humour remains much the same and values are defended in the face of changing circumstances.

Another aspect which remains constant is the physical environment. The coastline to the north of the city offers miles of sand dunes of near Arabian splendour. To the south, towering cliffs are at constant war with the changing moods of the North Sea.

The rural landscape west of Aberdeen is a challenge for any artist's palette. Late summer sees the upper valley of the Dee shimmer with speckled birch trees, and the ochre-green larches drooping ever lower. On Donside, a rusty yellow glow washes over fields of harvested corn and barley, broken only by narrow swathes of ancient woodlands. Winter's muted colours lie in wait. When the frozen Baltic breathes on the north-east, the air bites razor-sharp and lung-penetrating. When the wind is cold enough for snow – we call it 'sna caul'.

Bright winter sunlight compensates with remarkable clarity. All is crisp and sharp, as far as the eye can see; the granite sparkling in celebration of Aberdeen's other name, the 'Silver City'.

Is this too romantic a memory?

Of course it is. The mind is selective and recollections do warm with time, but the landscape, the city, its people and their ways, leave a lasting imprint which many carry for life. It would seem reasonable that such a place would hold on to its sons and daughters, but the 'wanderlust' was at work among my friends as we approached adult life. Many left the city, some for a career at sea, others to seek work in Australia, Canada or other far-off destinations. Even my constant primary-school friend and close companion, Isobel, left, eventually to settle in Miami, Florida. Yet closer, my brother, Tom, and his young wife, Mary, set off to a new life in British Columbia. I was to see them only a few times more in the years ahead.

Perhaps their going allowed me to stay; perhaps the landscape had finally won me over. Those of us who remain still respect the courage of those who left for a new life, while we carry our own 'what ifs?'. New lives they certainly established as, like previous generations of Scots, they took up the challenge of a fresh start far from home. What is abundantly clear is that each of these exiles retained an emotional link with their roots.

There was a simple way to express that tie to Scotland in a new community. If the opportunity was there, name it in tribute and fond memory of home. We see that now as we wonder at the many Scots place names which have been transplanted from our country to distant parts of the world. To discover among them the name 'Aberdeen' is to reveal evidence of a continuing link to this corner of Scotland. Others before me have shared strong reflections of a place.

I hold great respect for the generations of north-east Scots who set out on epic voyages to foreign parts. They faced enormous demands upon their courage and endurance. For many, it all began in this ancient city on the northern coast of Scotland.

In a less demanding way, I attempted to retrace their steps and repeatedly, throughout my journey, I met many who wanted to hear something of the history of the original Aberdeen. Perhaps personal reflections on the city have eased me towards tackling the more complex and centuries-old story of my birthplace. This was never going to be the easiest of challenges. However, once accepted, I was intrigued and humbled at the persistence of the city and the optimism of its citizens.

There's Aye A Something

Belcanny is foggin', wi' siller laid by,
Wi' byres fu' o' feeders an' pedigree kye.
Wi' horse in fine fettle for ploo or for harrow,
An' a' the teels needit fae binder to barrow;
The fire hoose an' steadin' sneck harled and hale,
Wi' boortree for lythe an' a gean at the gale;
A hillside o' bracken for beddin' the stots,
In hairst for the thackin' a gushet o' sprots;
The snod dykit feedle lies fair to the sun,
An' anither Nineteen's little mair nor begun;
He's lucky, Belcanny, his boolie rowes weel,
But aye there's a something – the wife is genteel.
Her fowk thocht a fairmer an unco come doon,
For a queyn that was teachin' an' raised i' the toon.
But though like the lave her ambitions were big,
She couldna say 'Na' till a laad wi' a gig;
An' soon they were baith sittin' cushioned an' saft,
An' passin' the peppermints up i' the laft.
An' faith she was thrang wi' her chuckens an' cheese,
Her eggs and her butter an' skepfu's o' bees;
An' better still, Hogmany hardly was by
Or the howdie was in, and she'd hippens to dry;
But aye there's a something, a mote on the meen,
She's great upon mainners – an' Sandy has neen.
He's roch an' unshaven till Sunday comes roon,
A drap at his nose, an' his pints hingin' doon;
His weskit is skirpit wi' dribbles o' kail,
He drinks fae his saucer, an' rifts owre his ale;
An' when he comes in fae the midden or moss
Her new – washen kitchie's as dubby' the closs.
She has her piana to dirl an' to thump,
But gie him for music a spring on the trump;

She's thankfu' for muckle, her doonsittin's fine,
The hoose an' the plenishin' just till her min';
But aye there's a something, the stob to the rose,
In spite o' a' tellin' – he blaws on his brose.
To haud them oonhappy would hardly be fair,
To ca' them ill – marrowed would anger them sair;
There's lots o' waur bodies, she'll freely alloo,
He's hearty an' kindly, baith sober an' foo;
He grudges her naething, be't sweeties or claes,
An' has for her hizzyship clappin' an' praise.
She's busy the but as a hen amon' corn
Gin noses need dichtin' or breekies are torn,
An' ben when the littlins need happin' or help,
To kiss or to cuddle, to scaul or to skelp.
They're like her in looks as a podfu' o' piz,
But dam't there's aye something – their mainners are his.

CHARLES MURRAY

Saskatchewan   South Dakota   Indiana   Ohio   Pennsylvania

Alberta

Montana

Idaho

Washington

California

Kentucky

Arkansas

West Virginia

Mississippi

Virginia   Florida   Jamaica   Antigua   Guyana

New Jersey   Maryland   Cape Breton   Aberdeen, Scotland

North Carolina

Australia

Sierra Leone   South Africa   Andaman Islands   Hong Kong   Tasmania

The name 'Aberdeen' spreads worldwide

A forest of trawler's masts,1953

replaced by oil supply vessels in the 1970s

ABERDEEN, SCOTLAND

Strandloopers, Bishops and Oil

The 'long ago' people of the north-east still intrigue local historians and archaeologists. The flint tools, pottery, crannogs, and standing stone circles from the pre-history of Aberdeenshire show that a variety of early settlers formed communities, hunted, fished, fought and worshipped with all the vigour and purpose of today.

'Strandloopers' were among the earliest and are so called because they worked the coastline, moving from one strand or spit of sand to the next. They harvested shellfish, dumping the discarded shells in large mounds or 'middens'. These distant people and others who farmed inland were in the north-east around 4,000 to 3,000 BC.

Much later, the same area was the domain of the Picts. Their history is still being pieced together, and they owed much of their culture to the influx and influence of Northern European and Baltic people.

It is said that the Pictish defeat of the Angles from the north of England, at Nechtansmere (north of Dundee) in AD 685, may have been one of the earliest indications that Scotland was showing a sense of basic nationhood. Most of Scotland would have become Anglia had the Picts been defeated. A proud and cultural people, as can be seen in their ancient carved stones, the Picts were to fade away as Christian influences came from the west.

Some claim that the Pictish spirit lives on in north-east folk – it may be seen in our stubborn and independent ways. Like the landscape, we seem stable, but we have a passion for music, song, debate and tales of adventure. Like the climate, our moods can alter.

The first mention of 'Aberdeen' is hard to trace. However, 'Aber-don' means 'at the mouth of the Don', 'Aber-da-aevin' is Gaelic for 'the outfall of two rivers', and in 1153 the Norse chieftain Eysteinn laid waste to a town on the coast which he called 'Aperdion'. The present city still lies on the coast

Aberdeen's other name, 'The Silver City'

between the rivers Dee and Don and so, by whatever name, Aberdeen has been in existence for a thousand years.

Ahead of the city lay many centuries of struggle and turbulence, often at the mercy of those who battled ruthlessly for territory and for power. These centuries saw Scotland appearing to tear itself apart, as it lost its royal line, challenged, reformed and restructured its church and tamely sold off its centuries of independence.

To summarise six or seven centuries of history is a task for the most serious of scholars. This writer makes no such professional claim! There will be no attempt to tackle this other than by a surface sweep of Aberdeen's long story. How did the city cope with these long and difficult years?

Like all sensible cities it focussed on progressing trading skills, increasing economic security and providing for its citizens. A challenge for the city fathers. With good fortune, they had a head start in 1179 when the city was granted a Royal Charter by William the Lion. The charter allowed city merchants to trade freely in all of Scotland's fairs and markets, exempt from the usual levy paid to the burgesses of other towns. What an advantage to the city's traders! The Royal Charter is still held in the city's vaults and is the oldest bestowed on any Scottish burgh.

In the 1200s, Carmelite, Dominican, Franciscan, Blackfriar and other missionaries came to the city. These religious orders established chapels, seminaries and fine residences. It was as if the north-east was 'the last great challenge' for Christianity in Scotland. The city is indebted to the arrival of these religious scholars who were to enhance the reputation of the north-east for many centuries. When we look today at St Machar Cathedral and St Nicholas Church, we should remember how it all began. A secure trading base with the Baltic countries and wider Europe ensured that medieval Aberdeen was bustling and successful. Bishops and merchants competed with each other to construct fine homes and centres for worship or trade.

Disaster struck, however, in 1244 when fire destroyed much of the timber-built town, yet this did allow the 1,500 citizens to replace what had been a warren of dreadful housing.

Barely a half century had passed when the city was occupied as Edward I of England sought revenge on Scotland. Many of the troubles of Scotland originated with its nobility, powerful figures who scrambled for power regardless of consequence. These nobles could not agree on a successor to the late Alexander of Scotland and invited Edward to choose on their behalf. He did so with the agreement that his man would become the 'Overlord of Scotland'. Edward chose John Balliol. However, when he summoned Balliol to gather troops to fight with him in France, Balliol refused with good reason, as Scotland and France were bound together under the 'Auld Alliance'.

A wintry
St Nicholas Church

The furious Edward punished Scotland severely, Aberdeen being but one of the burghs occupied by English troops. The consequences of Edward's actions were to come in the form of rebellion, championed by William Wallace and Robert the Bruce, and resulting in the Wars of Independence which raged across Scotland for some twenty years.

Aberdeen was supportive of the Scottish cause, especially as Robert the Bruce was a regular, and benevolent, visitor to the city. Victory over the English at Bannockburn in 1314 restored stability to the country, and Robert the Bruce rewarded Aberdeen for its support by granting the local burgesses the right to raise revenue from lands which he owned in the locality. This became the basis of today's Common Good Fund, where the collected rents are used for local purposes. Careful management of the Fund over six hundred years has served the city well, providing financial assistance for civic projects and 'entertainment expenses', such as those incurred during the visits of Winston Churchill and the Soviet President, Mikhail Gorbachev. Aberdeen may have been the first burgh in Scotland to establish a Common Good Fund, but it has been a centuries-old tradition which has benefitted many a Scottish town and city.

Robert the Bruce's death in 1329 hit Aberdeen very hard. His six-year-old son was obviously incapable of defending the country, and Edward III of England seized the opportunity to seek revenge for previous Scottish defiance. Once more, Scotland was in turmoil and Edward made a number of intrusions across the Border, his forces reaching as far north as Aberdeen. In the consequent battle, many citizens were massacred and the city put to the torch in 1336, the fire raging for six days. It is still regarded as the worst calamity in the city's long history. It was to be some years before a 'New Aberdeen' emerged from the ashes.

Was that an end of bloodshed and war? Not a chance. The nobles of Scotland had become very powerful and their greed for more land was insatiable.

One of the most troublesome was Donald 'Lord of the Isles', who took possession of much of the north-east and looked somewhat acquisitively at Aberdeen. In 1411 his army of ten thousand was defeated at Harlaw, less than twenty miles from the town. The slaughter was horrific. Many a local burn is called 'Redburn', such was the carnage on the battlefield.

Although the battle cost Aberdeen its Provost, Robert Davidson, many citizens and countless others from the east coast fought to repel the 'Lord of

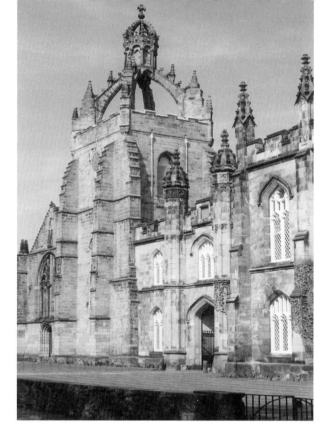

King's College,
one of the oldest
universities in the UK

the Isles' and the city survived once more and returned to relative stability. It was now in a position to consolidate itself as a major trading centre and a place of learning.

The church was growing in influence in the city, and the presence of bishops and other academics attracted scholars from around Europe. They were delighted to study in the seminaries of this north-east corner of Scotland. One of these was Bishop Elphinstone, who was to change so much in Aberdeen. In 1494, he founded King's College, the third university in Scotland which put Aberdeen firmly on the European map as a seat of learning. Education took another leap forward when a second university, Marischal College, was inaugurated in 1593. Now the city had the same number of universities as all of England!

The original College building occupied the site of the redundant Greyfriar's Monastery. The neo-Gothic frontage we see today was created much later in 1891. As a granite building, it is second in size only to El Escorial, Madrid.

In the sixteenth and seventeenth centuries, Aberdeen endured a sustained period of religious upheaval. In 1560, a law was passed in Scotland establishing Protestantism in direct opposition to the Catholic Church. This led to the savage and brutally confrontational reform of the Church.

The 'Reformation', as it is known, is well documented and was a dreadful time for the city as Scotland broke its 'Auld Alliance' with France. The change in relationship with Europe severely affected the merchants of Aberdeen but, even as full recovery seemed within reach, another event burst upon the scene in 1638. Charles the First sought to make Scotland worship according to the Episcopalian Church of England, the resulting resistance leading to the tragic years of the Covenanters and more bloodshed throughout the length and breadth of the country.

In time, Aberdeen saw through these years and returned to its own concerns. The fragile peace was not to last, however, and less than one hundred years later another turbulent event, the Jacobite Rebellion of 1745, saw Scotland once again steeped in blood. This time, we could blame no one but ourselves.

Many Aberdeenshire families were loyal to the cause of the Catholic Charles Edward Stuart and sacrificed their finest in the carnage at Culloden in 1746. The infamous Duke of Cumberland was accommodated in Aberdeen prior to marching north to Culloden, where he effectively destroyed Scotland's clan system.

About this time, Robert Gordon, an Aberdeen merchant who had made a fortune trading with the Baltic port of Danzig (now Gdansk, Poland), bequeathed most of his wealth to the founding of a 'hospital' for the education of the orphaned boys of Aberdeen. Robert Gordon's Hospital was a beacon in dark times. Even in the midst of political upheaval, here was a benefactor who established a centre for care and education. In the 1880s, it became Robert Gordon's College, with additional schools for the instruction of science and art; today, we know it as the Robert Gordon University.

In 1750, Aberdeen seemed to be maintaining focus on its own affairs, while all around was chaos. Some have criticised the city for alleged indifference to the 1745 Jacobite Rebellion, but Aberdeen, a city of merchants and scholars, had suffered enough of constant war and power seeking, and returned to what it did best – trading with the world.

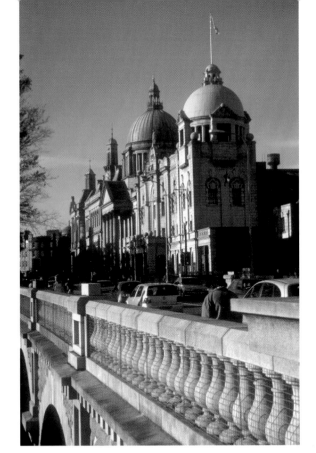

Granite balustrade
leads to H.M. Theatre

The 'Devil's Punchbowl' on Upper Deeside

From the standing-stones of the 'long-ago people' . . .

. . . . to the proud stones of Huntly Castle

Europe and the expanding markets of North America then played their part in the growing success of the city; global economy is not a new concept.

By 1748, a news sheet was produced to cover local events. Now called the *Press and Journal*, it is one of the oldest daily newspapers in the UK, reporting on the election of each of the many Presidents of the USA and the discovery of Australia.

Trade continued to expand and as it did so the city grew in size, the population exploding from six thousand in 1707 to a staggering sixty-three thousand by 1841.

In 1801, Union Bridge, at the time the largest civil engineering project in Europe, was constructed in a series of vast arches over the waters of the Denburn. This allowed the main thoroughfare, Union Street, to extend to a mile of magnificent granite buildings, seen by many as the birth of the 'Granite City'.

Granite and the north-east have had a long relationship. The elaborately decorated Marischal College, and even the fountains in Trafalgar Square, London, were hewn from that durable Aberdeen stone. Such was the demand for local granite, with Rubislaw and Kemnay quarries providing the paving for much of London and Odessa, that Aberdeen became a city of granite merchants, and vast fortunes were made.

Export of salted fish to Europe was still a major industry in Aberdeen, and it was soon complemented with the largest textile industry in Scotland, paper production, ship-building and, of course, the granite quarrying.

Ship-building skills in the city reached a peak in the 1860s, when a fleet

The 14th-century Brig o' Balgownie

of 'tea clippers' was constructed for the world's tea merchants, the most impressive vessel being the majestic *Thermopylae* which could sail to Melbourne in just sixty days!

This was a confident city – culturally and financially rich; secure in itself as it strode into the twentieth century. However, it was not to be the easiest period of history, as World Wars impacted so tragically; not once, but twice. In the 1940s, Aberdeen, conveniently close to occupied Europe, was a useful 'training run' for enemy bombers and suffered many night raids. I recall most of them.

In the 1950s, post-war recovery was slow throughout Europe and Aberdeen, in common with others, looked to a better and peaceful future. All seemed well, but the cost of quarrying granite became prohibitive and Aberdeen's vast trawling fleet was virtually wiped out by new restrictions and new fishing methods. Traditional industries were in serious decline and the livelihoods of many citizens were so threatened in the 1950s and 1960s that thousands left for better opportunities, travelling as far afield as Canada and Australia. How did the city cope?

As with most Scots, North-east folk have survived off the land or the sea for centuries, vulnerable to the whims of fate. And with many families seeing their loved ones head off to new challenges overseas, Charles Murray's phrase – 'there's aye a something' – was used once more with typical resignation.

However, destiny must have a conscience, because it smiled upon Aberdeen in the 1970s. The North Sea offered up oil, the city grasped this

Union Street, 1885

The Mercat Cross,
meeting-place of
medieval merchants

favour and today Aberdeen, with some justification, claims to be the 'oil capital' of Europe. Remarkably, it seems as if the flow of Aberdonians to North America has been reversed. Many American families have settled here, bringing skills and energy to the north-east. A new Aberdeen is forming: a city of around two hundred and twenty thousand, adapted to its present and favoured situation, but still very proud of its history.

As with all of Scotland, the past is within touch for those who pause and look around. Aberdeen is no different.

At the heart of the city stands the ancient Tolbooth which was granted its prison licence by Robert III in 1394. It was rebuilt in 1615 after severe gale damage, and in 1627 a belfry and spire were added. Its massive clock, which is still in use, dates from 1817.

To the west of the Tolbooth Tower lies the Town House, a splendid granite building which is of uncertain date, although there are records of repair work carried out in 1670 and rebuilding in 1729. The interior is resplendent with stately rooms, richly decorated with priceless chandeliers – some of them commissioned from the world-renowned crystal glass-making town of Waterford, Ireland.

Just beyond in the open space of the Castlegate stands the decorative Mercat Cross (1686), once the meeting place of Aberdeen's medieval merchants. The Brig o' Balgownie, dating from 1286, is Scotland's oldest medieval bridge and St Machar Cathedral survives from 1378. King's College (1494); the Bridge of Dee (1518); Provost Skene's House (1545); Provost John Ross's House (1710); St Andrew's Cathedral (1816); and St Mary's Cathedral (1860) are all within the city's boundaries.

The history of the north-east can also be glimpsed in its many castles: Craigievar, Corgarff, Drum, Crathes, Tolquhon, Kildrummy, Midmar, Castle Fraser, Balmoral (the Royal family's Scottish home) and the impressive ruins of Dunnottar Castle – the location of Mel Gibson's *Hamlet* – are but a few.

However, these imposing structures do not tell the whole story of countless generations. Our institutions and individuals have influenced the histories of other places worldwide, and continue to do so.

In 1497, the University of Aberdeen founded the first Chair of Medicine in the English-speaking world, and five centuries later it developed the MRI scanner. Further afield in Asia, Thomas Blake Glover, from the north-east, was one of the founders of Japan's industrial revolution and had a central role in establishing Mitsubishi.

Perhaps that is the true story of not only Aberdeen, but all of Scotland, as scholars, merchants, industrialists and entrepreneurs achieved success at home or sought new challenges abroad. In centuries of trading, our greatest export has probably been people. From bar-room to boardroom, the cry has been heard: 'Scotsmen, damned Scotsmen, and Aberdonians!' More complimentary to the essential Scot is the praise that we are 'adjustable to needs and circumstances, stubbornly persistent'.

That stubborn persistence is reflected in the histories of the communities which I had the good fortune to visit on my travels. Each has required strength of character to cope with changing circumstances, each has a unique personality; all are connected by a shared heritage.

'Tell me about the other Aberdeens.'

The many flights and miles on the road may still confuse me, but recollections of the Aberdeens are clear and lasting.

It is time we heard their stories.

Craigievar Castle,
Aberdeenshire

Marischal College, a proud feature of the 'Granite City' skyline

Downtown Aberdeen, Matawan

New Jersey and my first view of its stylish timber homes

ABERDEEN, NEW JERSEY, U.S.A.

Quakers, Propriety and Cranberry Sauce

The ninety-five-thousand-mile journey to large and small, forgotten and fascinating, strange and exotic locations world-wide begins in New Jersey, USA. It may well be the oldest Aberdeen beyond the shores of Scotland.

For thousands of years this was the land of the Lenni Lanape, whose territory was to become New Jersey. European settlement began in 1650 when the Dutch purchased the south side of Raritan Bay. In 1664, the entire area came under English possession and the native Indians moved West. Their legacy lives on in names such as 'Mohingson', 'Luppatatong', 'Matawan' and 'Raritan'.

During my investigations, I quickly discovered that the birth of New Jersey is one of the most complicated of any of the new territories in America. I needed help! Ed Fitzgerald and John McGinty, two helpful and knowledgeable residents who I met in New Jersey, took me through the complex background which led to the founding of their Aberdeen.

It all came about in the 1680s due to the then Governor Barclay encouraging Scots to 'come over' to this new and growing colony. Many responded and a small farming community was established just beyond the settlement of Matawan. The farming Freehold Township was mostly settled by Scots Presbyterians and Quakers, among them John Reid and George Keith from Aberdeen, Scotland. Keith, a Presbyterian clergyman, became very involved in the community and it is reasonable to assume that he played a part in naming the small township Aberdeen.

Much later, the distinctly rural Aberdeen was absorbed into the larger downtown area of Matawan Borough and was obliged to change its name. It waited for three hundred years until it could once again call itself Aberdeen Township.

The forging of New Jersey is a complex story and a return back through

New Jersey sketch

time reveals more of the difficult and demanding times which beset those who had left their homeland.

The seventeenth century provides a typical example of how European interests elbowed and squared up to each other to establish a foothold in this most promising of continents. The English Crown had ancient claim to the ownership and sovereignty of North America, based on discoveries of 1497. However, the claims lay dormant throughout England's Civil War, the rule of Oliver Cromwell and the overthrow of Charles I in 1649.

The 'trouble at home' left the territory around New Jersey open to the Dutch and the Swedes, and they established settlements on the Delaware and the Hudson. By 1660, the monarchy in England was restored and Charles II was declared King. The English Restoration, as it is known, had taken place. Now was the time to deal with unfinished business in America and Charles II provided the Duke of York with sufficient force to re-take the New Jersey territory, and declare it under the 'laws and sovereignty' of Britain.

This period in Britain's history was a time of corrupt 'wheeling and dealing' as various power groups sought to curry favour with the incoming Charles II. As in all such situations, many were out of favour and faced persecution; the wisest sought an escape route.

Among the most vulnerable were the 'Quakers', a popular term of insult used to describe every member of the Society of Friends. Many of this highly organised sect of around 50,000 sought refuge and a new life free from persecution by sailing to America. Their 1620 voyage on the *Mayflower* planted the name of the English naval town of 'Plymouth' on east-coast America and they were to play a significant role in the settlement of New Jersey.

Under English ownership, the lands of East Jersey were up for auction by the trustees of Sir George Cartaret's widow, Lady Elizabeth Cartaret. So, for the grand sum of £3,400, a group of twelve men, headed by William Penn, became the new proprietors and were allowed the right of government. These original twelve agreed to add twelve more voices to their group and among this new group of East Jersey landowners were Scots.

Robert Barclay, a Scots Quaker, was one of the new proprietors and he was instrumental in attracting a steady flow of Scots to an area on the coast called 'East New Jersey'. Barclay saw his new territories as a place of refuge for persecuted Scots – not only Scots but others who wished to leave the troubles of Scotland could begin a new life. More than 6,000 Quakers migrated to Pensylvannia and almost 2,000 to East New Jersey.

In 1682, Barclay was elected governor of East New Jersey and worked at persuading relatives and others that this territory could become a New Albion or New Scotland. More than anyone, Barclay ensured that what was later to become the State of Jersey would have a long and lasting connection with Scotland.

Among those who joined his enterprise were Sir John Gordon of Durno, Sir Robert Gordon of Gordonstown, the Gordons of Straloch, Sir Ewan Cameron of Lochiel and Forbeses of Aquorthes.

Another Scot to seize the opportunity to settle in America was George Scott, Laird of Pitlochie, Fife. With wisdom, he requested that Presbyterian prisoners be turned over to him as bonded servants so that he could sail to America and establish a colony where they could pursue their faith. This was agreed and, on 1 July 1685, the *Henry and Francis* set sail for New Jersey with two hundred souls aboard. Setting out from Leith (near Edinburgh), the ship called at Aberdeen to conclude all business arrangements.

The fifteen-week crossing of the Atlantic was devastating as fever and poor conditions claimed the lives of almost half the passengers. Among those who perished were the Laird of Pitlochie and his wife. Thus, by a cruel twist of Fate, the bonded servants arrived as free men and women.

While they were at sea, 400 acres of land were granted by the proprietors of East Jersey to a Mr Stephen Warne, a merchant from Dublin, and his son, Thomas. Their land was called 'Warne's Neck'. With the friendship of Thomas Warne, the newly landed immigrants purchased land on the banks of Matawan Creek, naming their new settlement 'Aberdeen'. There they would enjoy the naval protection of England, and yet live under their own traditional laws in a Scottish colony. An odd but welcome arrangement!

By the eighteenth century, the settlement of Scots had expanded north along the creek. What had been a farming community became a fishing port and common agreement among traders led to the name being changed to 'Middletown Point'.

Middletown Point was the principal shipping centre for the entire area, the creek boasting an average depth of twelve feet and being wide enough to accommodate ocean-going vessels at its many docks. Traders and suppliers enjoyed a peaceful existence, and many fortunes were made. However, all this was shattered when Middletown Point became a strategic centre during the American War of Independence. Legends lived, fought and died here.

Philip Freneau, 'The Poet of the Revolution'; 'Old Corn King' and his son, Major John Burrowes; General David Forman; and Major Thomas Hunn, commander of the local militia, are among New Jersey's heroes.

Many reprisal raids were conducted by the Crown forces as Middletown Point was perceived as 'a hotbed of treasonous activity'.

Following the ravages of war and the gaining of independence, the post-revolution period saw considerable growth in industry and shipping. Soon, there were mills, a tannery, pottery, brickyard and potash factory. In 1834, *Gordon's Gazetteer* described Middletown Point thus,

It lies on a bank elevated about fifty feet above the stream, a marsh on the opposite side, contains a Presbyterian church, from 75 to 100 buildings, 8 or 10 stores, 4 taverns and a grist mill. Large quantities of pork, rye, corn, cordwood and truck are thence sent to New York.

Steam navigation replaced the more sedate sail as freight and passengers moved rapidly back and forth to New York. Consequently, the creek silted

An early
morning start

up and became unusable. Nevertheless, the township prospered and other industries developed. By 1830, the Farmers and Merchants Bank was founded and for thirty-four years it was the only bank in Monmouth County.

In 1865, to avoid postal confusion with Middletown, the burgh of Middletown Point altered its name to 'Matawan'. Much later, in 1977, wishing to retain local identity and control of civic matters in an expanded group of burghs, the small farming township which had been absorbed into Matawan returned to its previous name, 'Aberdeen'. In respect to both historic communities, the railroad station is called 'Matawan–Aberdeen'.

Aberdeen Township today has around twenty thousand citizens and is one of a group of small independent communities nestling in this beautiful corner of New Jersey. The township is neat, tidy and compact – reminiscent of a small market town.

I was struck by the many fine timber buildings, decoratively painted in muted greys with features highlighted in white. The shore is close at hand and from there it is possible to see New York across the bay. Within forty minutes, as the thousands of commuters who take the train to the Big Apple each day will testify, it is possible to be in downtown Wall Street or Times Square. If visiting New York, I would seriously consider staying in

Aberdeen and travelling into the city each day, but not for the food. Aberdeen has many fine places to eat and in a local diner I sampled one of the finest clam chowders ever.

The surrounding landscape is green and pleasantly rural, and this is one community which deserves a return visit, if only to meet up again with Mark Coren, Ed Fitzgerald, John McGinty, Brian Dougherty and the many others who made my visit so special.

This is a special place for the historian, too. The past is all around and Matawan Creek, the landing place for those early settlers, runs alongside the town. The proximity of the shoreline, which faces east towards Europe, conjures up images of generations of immigrants arriving on the shores of this land. As I looked beyond Raritan Bay from the harbour area of nearby Keyport, for a moment or two I was sure that I could see sailing ships and the waves of optimistic souls.

Though close to the frantic pace of larger cities, Aberdeen has retained a gentle atmosphere, in no small way due to the efforts of the local Township Council. Mayor Sobel invited me to one of their meetings and I saw US democracy at work. Now that was something! Local residents were invited to ask questions and 'genuine exchange' was part of the process. Real accountability to real people. I was very impressed.

New Jersey, the 'quiet backwater State'? Certainly not. New Jersey, the Garden State has had more than its fair share of innovative thinkers and can claim many firsts. America's first brewery opened in Hoboken in 1642. The first organised game of baseball was held at Elysian Field, Hoboken, 1846. The oldest operating lighthouse in the USA is at Sandy Hook. Elizabeth Lee of New Egypt boiled some damaged cranberries and came up with the first cranberry sauce. Thanks Elizabeth. And let's not forget *Jaws*!

We all know about the great white shark, thanks to the movie, but did you know that in 1916 one such terrible fish did, in fact, attack and kill along the New Jersey coast, before finally entering Matawan Creek where it took the lives of a number of young victims?

From the Appalachians to the lakes, forests and coastline, New Jersey is a jewel of a state. It is a time-capsule of American history, with numerous historical centres and associated events. Here, for more than three hundred years, a township has survived and may claim to be the oldest Aberdeen beyond the mother city in Scotland.

ABERDEEN, OHIO, U.S.A.

A Welshman, a Squire and Turkeys

This Aberdeen had its beginnings in the late 1700s in Brown County, hard on the southern border of Ohio, looking across the Ohio River towards Kentucky. The State of Ohio has natural assets of good farmland, timber and coal and this attracted settlers in the eighteenth and nineteenth centuries.

However, to research the history of Aberdeen, Ohio, is to meet again and again the influence of Nathan Ellis. A Welshman, Ellis grew up in neighbouring Pennsylvania, where his parents had settled in 1750. As a successful young man, he made his way down the Ohio River looking for a place to put down roots. His location chosen, Ellis laid out plans for a new town, setting aside substantial plots for his mansion and warehouse. A forward-looking person, Ellis turned his mind to various projects. He planted the first orchard in Brown County and operated the first ferry from Ohio to Kentucky. His influence is legendary and his commitment to the community was such that he served as Justice of the Peace until his death

Ohio Valley Mill
receipt of 1914

in 1819. Townships like Aberdeen, Ohio, need people with the drive and foresight of Nathan Ellis. They are the making of such places.

Around 1788, Matthew Campbell of Aberdeen, Scotland, crossed the river from Brook's Bar, purchased a tract of land in Brown County, and committed himself to the new town and to neighbouring Huntington. While it is generally accepted that he gave the town its name, others claim that it was named by James Edwards, also from Aberdeen, Scotland. Edwards fought in America's Revolutionary War, was given land in Ohio Valley and settled here. Either way, the connection back to Scotland is very powerful.

The histories of Aberdeen and Huntington are closely related, Aberdeen being laid out in July 1816, some time after Huntington.

A small town on the banks of the Ohio with a long way to go!

I drove into Aberdeen from the south side of the river by way of Maysville, Kentucky. Nowadays, it is easy to cross the Ohio on an immense modern bridge, but it was not always that simple. For some years local schoolchildren went to school in Maysville and were forced to cross the Ohio by ferry. Eventually, a log schoolhouse was built on the land of Ewan Campbell in 1817. The first teacher was a Scot, a Mr Calderwood, who received $2.50 per student for a period of three months.

With Scots and education goes religion, no matter where. In 1800, the Revd. Wood began conducting Baptist services, and there was Methodist worship at the house of James Dennis in Huntington. A twenty-year period of church building started with the Bethlehem Church at Slickaway Creek in 1829. This was followed the next year by the Presbyterian Church and Aberdeen's own church, the M. E. Church, was completed in 1845.

The town was expanding.

By the mid-1800s, Aberdeen, so dependent on the river for transportation all the way to St Louis, had grown into a township of 'two dry goods stores, two blacksmith shops, one wagon shop, one tannery, a hotel, two livery stables, a lumber and coal yard, a school and five churches'.

Aberdeen–Huntington had some remarkable characters, not the least being Squire Massie Beasley. He purchased Valley Mansion and served there as Justice of the Peace for many years. Valley Mansion had been built by Nathan Ellis in 1799 and in it Squire Beasley married over three thousand couples, few of whom possessed a licence, and most of whom had no parental approval. In those days, that was a pretty serious business, but it was profitable!

Squire Beasley was merely continuing the tradition of his predecessor Thomas Shelton who performed twenty-five thousand marriages from 1822 to 1869. Together, they earned Aberdeen the reputation of being 'the Gretna Green of America'. The original Gretna Green in Scotland is still popular with young couples from other countries who take advantage of Scotland's generosity in 'matters of the heart'.

There were problems, of course. Couples married by Squire Beasley (many of them were escaping slaves from the South) did not have the authority of American Law. After the Civil War, therefore, many widows did not qualify for a war widows pension. It took an Act of Congress to rectify this legal oversight.

Agriculture, logging and coal mining were the mainstay of Brown County for many years and companies such as the Ohio Valley Mill Co. employed local people. Massive logs made their way down the Ohio River, yet that same river which provided such useful transportation was also a constant threat to the community.

In 1913, the flatland of Aberdeen was badly flooded, the streets awash to a depth of many feet, damaging historic properties such as the White House Tavern, which had been owned by Matthew Campbell and Nathan Ellis. Despite recurring flooding in 1937, the town continues to flourish, with many of the original families still around. Names like Ellis, Campbell, Powers, Gallacher and Stewart are built into the origins of this Aberdeen.

The marriage of two
Scottish place names

Until recently, this rich farming area was tobacco growing country and I met up with Mike who showed me his vast tobacco barn. It is a huge building with slatted timber walls to allow the warm autumn air to blow through and dry the green leaves of tobacco. They would have hung from three or four storeys of horizontal poles.

The poles are still there but that industry has all but gone and Mike's vast barn has become yet another part of the history of Ohio. A real 'baccychewin' character, Mike now makes a wonderful array of fishing lures and ingenious turkey-callers. The dense woods around here are home to native American turkey and, in answer to the female-sounding turkey-caller, the male turkey is hastened to his end with thoughts on other matters. It is an unfair world!

In town, I met Kay Haag who has worked tirelessly to develop the Museum and, small as it is, it is a treasure house of this very historic township.

Valuable research is being carried out by the Aberdeen–Huntington Township Museum and the collection of old documents and artefacts will keep Kay and her colleagues busy for many a year to come. The Museum produces a publication called *The Sampler* and it is a fascinating record of Aberdeen's history.

To be in Aberdeen, Ohio, is to be aware of the mighty Ohio River. Here it is wide, deep and fast flowing. It forms a natural boundary between Ohio and Kentucky. This is part of the Mason–Dixon Line, so familiar to Civil War historians since, during the Civil War, many slaves made their way from Kentucky to Ohio. Along the northern side of the river there was a network of secret basement hiding places in homes and inns, from where these escaping slaves could head off even as far as Canada. This incredible system was called the 'Underground Railway' and many local folk, despite the risks, were willing to hide and assist runaway escapees.

Today, steep roads descend from densely wooded countryside to the main street, and beyond, to the riverbank. This is a river town with a number of conserved brick built buildings. A real find. The river itself has an awesome presence.

At the invitation of local character John R. Mitchell, I returned south over the bridge to Maysville, Kentucky. He had arranged a splendid meal at an exclusive club, owned by a generous Irishman in Maysville. John R. had his own tale to tell of great, great grandparents, by name of Kirk, who came

Aberdeen Ohio's favourite tool shop

Downtown Aberdeen, Ohio

Interesting use of an old tobacco barn

The home of Captain John Campbell, builder of river steamboats

'Fancy some fishing, Mike?'

from Scotland in the 1730s. The Scottish link is never hard to find. From Maysville, I looked back at Aberdeen and suspected that few American citizens appreciate the depth of history which is contained in small townships like this.

I left Aberdeen, Ohio, with knowledge that in communities like this there is genuine history. Some of Aberdeen's domestic buildings have been occupied for more than two hundred years. Among the earliest land to be settled in Ohio, this town has much to offer those who wish to delve into the past of a hard-won river community. The word 'Ohio' is Iroquois for 'beautiful' and in the Buckeye State there is much to value, in particular, the efforts of those who are stewards of the centuries-old story of Aberdeen.

If passing, a stop here is well worth it. Mike may even take you fishing.

ABERDEEN, INDIANA, U.S.A.

The Gillespies, Sunday School and a Casino

Further along the Ohio River and south west of Cincinnati is the lovely town of Rising Sun. The journey along the banks of that mighty river revealed again just how heavily wooded a region this is. Not until after Cincinnati did the landscape open up and Rising Sun come into view. A township of quaint streets and attractive houses, it soon provided me with the evidence which I was seeking. In under thirty minutes, driving through rolling farmland, I came to a crossroads and found Aberdeen.

Not much is left of this small place, but Jim Dorrell soon intrigued me with its history. Jim has lived here for all of his ninety years or more and has faithfully written down the story of Aberdeen. Although only a few houses remain, this was at one time a lively and very thriving farming village. Back in the 1880s, Brooks Store stood at the crossroads. There were a few houses, but the place had no name.

That all changed when the Gillespie family arrived from Scotland. They settled on the rich farmland and called the village 'Aberdeen'. The Gillespies had a reputation as superb gunsmiths, famed for the locally prized 'Gillespie Muzzle-loader Gun'.

In 1904, the road through the crossroads was altered when a bridge was built to allow easier access to John Woods Store. As a consequence, Aberdeen grew in size and soon had a few more additions to the original buildings. There was the Black Horse Tavern, the grocery store and the post office, run by Bruce Bascom in partnership with Jake Meyers. Much later, ownership transferred to the Dorrells who had the store and post office until about 1920.

This self-contained community had a blacksmith shop, sawmill, buggy shop, broom shop, schoolhouse, church and two grocery stores. Farming people, unlike city dwellers, can feed and water themselves and Jim recalls very few trips into Rising Sun as a child, since they had a small acreage on which they grew crops and vegetables, and kept a few chickens and hogs. In addition, they planted, harvested and dried their own tobacco: they had all they needed in Aberdeen!

He has memories of 'horse-shoe pitching' beside the Grandma Rand's home, visits to the cream-testing station and quiet summer days at the Old Murray Branch Schoolhouse. Jim reflects upon those years with great warmth. Years when the old Hodapp Farm produced fine cider, when Martha and Viola Heath owned a loom which wove beautiful rugs and carpets and when Francis Emery was the village paper-hanger, making every house a palace for $1 per room!

Sitting in the sun with old Mr Dorrell, I heard of these times and could feel myself drifting backwards through the years to what must have been an idyllic childhood in a gentle rural landscape. It took little leap of the imagination to transport myself to a meeting in Aberdeen, 3 May, 1898.

The gathering was called for the purpose of organising a Sunday School. After singing 'All Hail the Power of Jesus' name', the meeting was put into the hands of Mr Elwood Houze and it was instantly agreed that the Sunday School would be held five days later on 8th May. Decision making, Indiana style!

Irene Bovard recalls:

'The attendance was good and the collections generous. We met inside an enclosure, the youngsters sitting on planks of green timber resting on blocks of wood.'

Sadly, those times have gone and today Aberdeen is all but a ghost town. Folks around here still farm, but on a larger scale – the lush, green landscape dotted with their dairy herds.

It was a delight to meet Mr Dorrell and submit to the evocative tales of his childhood in what must have been a very friendly community, but I had to return to Rising Sun.

This, the closest town to old Aberdeen is another historic gem, nestling on the banks of the mighty Ohio River. Anchored here is the *Grand Victoria*, a four-storey paddle-steamer. This wonderful vessel was brought up from St Louis and is a vast floating casino!

The owner, Ynez Taylor, invited me aboard and I was boggle-eyed at the flashing one-arm bandits, spinning roulette wheels, colourful decor and at the amount of money vanishing down the card tables. A concern for any Aberdonian!

The evening was capped by a very special happening. After dark, the Grand Victoria moved elegantly out to mid-stream, its huge paddle wheel churning the waters of the now black Ohio. Care was taken not to cross the centre of the river lest it entered the waters on the Ohio side, where gambling is illegal and the consequences expensive.

Some minutes into the short voyage, the lights of an equally large paddle-steamer were seen moving elegantly over the water on the Ohio side. Great excitement erupted on board since this was the *Mississippi Queen*, a vast touring vessel which was making its way back home to the Deep South. As the two brightly illuminated 'ladies of the river' slid by each other, they exchanged greetings and the riverbanks echoed with the rich, full-bodied exchange of powerful horns. I can hear it still, deep and resonant.

Back in the casino, the visitors were having a great time and had no reluctance in contributing to the local economy. That is how it works here – the local community benefits from a proportion of casino revenue. New roads, lighting, sports facilities, recreation parks for youngsters and many other amenities are aided by the *Grand Victoria*'s profits. Now, wouldn't that be something for us to think about in Scotland? I can see such a vessel on the River Dee, close to the Duthie Park.

But this is Rising Sun, Indiana, not Riverside Drive, Aberdeen!

In this beautiful town, I spent some time in one of the most comprehensive local museums I have ever seen. Here, the complete story of Aberdeen and other communities in Ohio County have been lovingly reconstructed. This museum is a 'must' for serious researchers of late nineteenth-century rural America.

Jim Dorrell brought to life the Aberdeen of his childhood, and in this serene corner of Indiana, life remains gentle and very tempting. The arrival of the Gillespie family from Scotland, along with names such as Jamieson, Buchanan, Scott, McHenry, Murray and McPherson show that many a Scot lingered here. Had the time been available, I also might have dallied in the 'Hoosier State', as it is nicknamed. However my journey was only just beginning and many more Aberdeens were waiting to be visited.

And more Aberdonians to meet!

Aberdeen, South Dakota, U.S.A.

Sioux, Oz and a Haircut

South Dakota, a territory of glacial valleys and hills, has been inhabited for almost three thousand years, but it was not until the 1700s that white fur traders met the Dakota Sioux and the Arikara.

Colin Campbell ran a trading post on the Elm River around 1822, his relationship with the local Indians based on mutual respect and trust. In 1868, the Teton Sioux, Lakota Sioux, Cheyenne, Arapaho and other tribes secured possession of the Black Hills by treaty; a sacred place of physical and spiritual renewal. However, rumours persisted of great wealth to be found in the 'Paha Sapa' Indian territory of the Black Hills and these were confirmed when George Armstrong Custer returned from an expedition into the Black Hills, with tales of gold.

The temptation of untold wealth was too great and there was a frantic rush of prospectors in their thousands pouring into what was, by Government treaty, Indian territory. This was the scenario which led to years of conflict in the Indian lands. Dakota is a Sioux word, meaning 'alliance of friends'. Sadly, the tragic events of this period denied its true meaning.

The Sioux defended their lands and their way of life, as all would, and the Indian Wars which followed lasted for more than a decade. This terrible time is well documented and, on both sides, the loss of life was tragic. However, South Dakota continued to hold out enticing prospects to those who had the courage to cross the Plains.

In 1862, the US Government promised free land to anyone who could clear 160 acres, work it and live on it for five years. Such an offer drew large numbers of settlers to South Dakota and twelve such pioneers founded the settlement of Grand Crossing, where the Chicago, Milwaukee, St Paul and Pacific Railroad intersected the North Western Railway right-of-way.

Here, the Rice Brothers and Boyden set up a post office and store. The location of Aberdeen was to be very close to this spot in the north-east of South Dakota.

These early settlers were remarkable people, as Amelia Knight expressed:

> The men and women who would one day push out on to the Great Plains faced a beautiful, cruel and unforgiving landscape. They were mostly ordinary people, eager to make something extraordinary of the land and of themselves. It took all the courage they could muster.

In Brown County, the chosen site for the new town of Aberdeen was a few miles from Grand Crossing. In true pioneer style, the store and post office were moved to this new location. Later that same year, the first train arrived and the post office opened.

1881 was a significant year for the town of Aberdeen. Charles H. Prior, town site agent for the Chicago, Milwaukee and St Paul Railroad, selected a site for a new town on behalf of his company. The railroad president, Alexander Mitchell, named it 'Aberdeen' in tribute to his native city in Scotland. The Alexander Mitchell Library, which stands on Kline Street, was funded by Andrew Carnegie, a friend and customer of Mitchell. It was the only 'Carnegie Library' in the USA not named after its founder. Instead, it was a fitting tribute to the Scot who had brought the name 'Aberdeen' to South Dakota.

The Freeman Bros supplied the
needs of a growing farming community

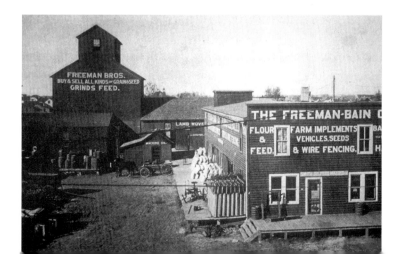

A typical 'Highlands District' mansion

My arrival in Aberdeen revealed little of its dramatic beginnings. I saw a large university city, wide avenues and little evidence of those early days. However, I found out much more about the 1880s when I met up with enthusiastic historians of that period.

On 4th August, 1881, the *Dakota Pioneer*, published by John H. Drake, came off the press, hotly followed by the *Aberdeen Republican* some hours later. This was a fast-growing, energetic community with a voracious reader's appetite! It is now served by the *Aberdeen American News* and *The Comet*. The publisher of the *American News* today is Adrian Pratt, a Scot.

Railroad companies feature strongly in pioneer communities and Aberdeen was no different. It soon became known as 'Hub City', in recognition of the network of rail lines converging in and around the large warehouses, which supplied essential goods to the region. As many as forty trains per day passed through the town.

Farm machinery stockists, food suppliers, flour mills, brick and wagon factories, and foundry premises all contributed to the rapid expansion of this part of South Dakota.

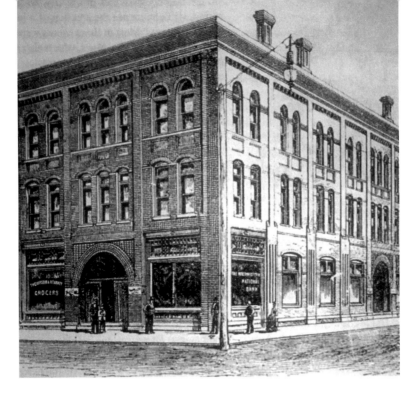

The Northwestern National Bank, 1889
(now the Dacotah Prairie Museum)

Receiving its city charter in 1883, Aberdeen enjoyed a steady expansion and a century later it has grown beyond the dreams of those early settlers. Today, it is a city of around twenty-five thousand citizens, home to Northern State University and numerous industrial enterprises, such as the FMC Corporation and 3M. A multi-cultural heritage is reflected in the many churches, representing a variety of denominations, and nearby are the self-sustaining communities of the Hutterite people.

Aberdeen was also home to two exceptional men – Mr Zietlow and Mr Baum. J. L. Zietlow built and operated the world's first automatic telephone dialling system. To recognise his achievement, the Telephone Pioneer Museum contains the largest collection of independent telephone company exhibits in the USA, dating from 1886.

L. Frank Baum lived in Aberdeen from 1888 to 1891, when he ran a store and a newspaper, but he is more famous as the author of *The Wonderful Wizard of Oz*. It is claimed that the droughts, the tornadoes and the strong-willed women of South Dakota are built into the story. In fact, the killing of the 'wicked witch' by drenching her with fresh water, is locally regarded as an echo of how the farmers wished they could deal with the evil of drought. Frank Baum's work is celebrated at Storybook Land, a large recreation centre in Wylie Park. This wonderful facility contains many fairy-tale features, including all the well-known characters and settings from the Land of Oz.

This, I just had to see for myself. In temperatures of over ninety degrees, I found myself saying, 'Hello,' to the Scarecrow, the Lion and the Tin Man. Even more childlike, I found myself skipping along the 'Yellow Brick Road' with reckless abandon. Old fool! It was a real fun afternoon with young and old sharing in this celebration of Oz literature at Wylie Park. All too soon, I had to head off to the outskirts of town. Ice-cream in one hand, burger in the other, I said my farewells to Dorothy and went off to meet Art Buntin and his friends.

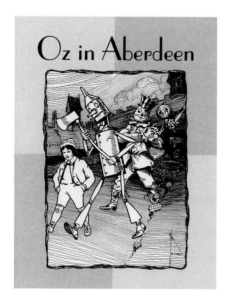

Wonder if he ever got
to the other Aberdeens?

In 1981, Brown County and Aberdeen Landmark Commission established Centennial Village as a tribute to the formative days of their town. This wonderful historic village recreates a typical pioneer atmosphere with great authenticity. Art, Don and Les are members of the hard-working group that has been instrumental in recreating this small Western township, which dates back to the 1880s.

Throughout the 1880s and 1890s town business expanded. It was originally conducted in sod huts and tents, but these were eventually replaced by timber-framed structures. Many of these original wooden buildings were moved to Centennial Village from other locations.

I ambled along the wooden sidewalks, impressed at the careful manner in which each property has been lovingly furnished with artefacts of the time. I marvelled at the livery stables, general store, old schoolhouse, saloon, telegraph office, boarding house and much more. After weeks on the road, I was glad to visit the authentic 1880s barber's shop, where Don Gisi gave me a much needed trim! Thanks, Don.

Being in this old pioneer village, and swaggering into the saloon by the low swing-doors, was like being on the set of a genuine Hollywood western movie. Aberdeen works hard at maintaining recollections of its past, and the Dacotah Prairie Museum is yet another centre dedicated to telling the story of the land and those who lived upon it. Sue Gates, Museum Director, Brenda Moore, Director of Tourism and Adrian Pratt treated me to a wonderful evening where they expressed genuine fondness of their city and an awareness of its Scottish connection. They made me humbly proud of my north-east roots.

It is all too easy to forget that this large modern city sits in the centre of a vast and relatively untouched landscape. *The Town in the Frog Pond,* the title of a book by Don Artz, is a fair description of Aberdeen since the region beyond the city is dotted with countless small ponds and water holes. Out there is Sand Lake National Wildlife Refuge, a haven for snow geese, Canada geese and thousands of migratory wildfowl. This area of marshes, forests and grassland is also home to striped skunk, red foxes, deer and the much-sought-after ring-necked pheasant. To the visitor it is a timeless landscape, with local wildlife much as it was, which I can vouch for, after my walk in the tall grasses. In the blink of an eye, something stung my forearm. By the time I reached town, my arm looked alarmingly swollen.

The staff at the Medical Centre pumped me with antibiotics, casually

'Careful with those clippers, Don!'

adding, 'It was a buffalo fly, we've had lots of them this year.' I shrugged the discomfort aside. Yes, those Scots pioneers were tough!

My time in Aberdeen, South Dakota, passed all too rapidly and I felt that there was much more to explore here in this large city with a lot of character, getting on with its busy life in the heart of the vast Great Plains. The culture and way of life of the Sioux nation may have gone, but the people of Coyote State have rediscovered the meaning of 'alliance of friends'. Mayor Hopper and his colleagues provided ample evidence that they just love folks to visit. Especially when you arrive in this Aberdeen from another Aberdeen.

ABERDEEN, MARYLAND, U.S.A.

Crossroads, Tobacco and Railroads

Without trading routes and railroads, Aberdeen, Maryland, may not have become the fine city which it is today. Here at the head of Chesapeake Bay, the original walkways were Indian trails that criss-crossed the wooded valleys and followed the many creeks and rivers which spill into the ocean. By the 1700s, farmers and planters settled here, grew and harvested tobacco and rolled their barrels along the old trails to shipping points. The continuous use of these trails established clearly defined routes, many of which became significant in the history of Harford County. The largest of these was the famous Post Road, running north to the city of Philadelphia and south to Baltimore and Washington.

Tobacco shipped to overseas markets increased the importance of landing places and Swan Creek was soon one of the busiest in the region. From here, roads went off in all directions to plantations and township. One crossed the Post Road on land owned by the Hall family. This intersection was called 'Hall's Cross Roads' and became the meeting place of many a trader who wished to rest in the tavern or have running repairs carried out at the blacksmith's shop. Life seemed positive, satisfying and, for the inn-keepers, undoubtedly profitable!

Dramatically, all that was to change when Thomas Jefferson drafted the Declaration of Independence in 1776. The result was the long struggle to free Maryland and neighbouring States from British colonization. After terrible sacrifice and conflict, the thirteen original colonies were finally liberated in 1789. Harford County saw no battle on its soil, but its citizens supported the cause of freedom. Hall's Cross Roads welcomed many troops, including La Fayette on his way to the battle at Yorktown.

After gaining independence, the region prospered. In this air of self-confidence many new settlers came to share in the riches of Maryland soil.

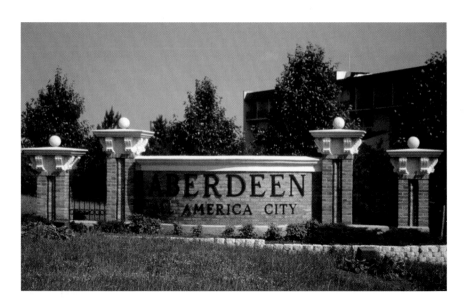

Welcome to an 'All America City'

Still standing in Aberdeen, Maryland, is this historic railroad station

This traveller
needs to
be re-shod!

Aberdeen, Maryland, excels in elegant avenues

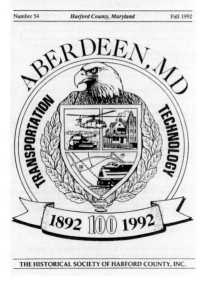

THE HISTORICAL SOCIETY OF HARFORD COUNTY, INC.

Aberdeen
Maryland's
proud crest

There was an upsurge in agricultural productivity in the early 1780s and, by 1788, Maryland was a recognised state and growing fast.

Inevitably, the cry went up for a more efficient transportation system and the Baltimore and Port Deposit Railroad came to Hall's Cross Roads in the early 1800s. With the railroad came the new stationmaster, Mr Winston from Scotland, and this marked the birth of Aberdeen, Maryland.

Mr Winston occupied a house just west of the cross-roads, and this became the first stopping station in the area. He named it 'Aberdeen'. The name stuck and soon it became a vital loading point for produce bound for Baltimore and Philadelphia.

Railroad expansion was the making of Aberdeen. The Baltimore and Port Deposit may have been the first track through town in 1831, but others were soon on their way. Mergers took place and this original small railroad company joined the larger Philadelphia, Wilmington and Baltimore (PW & B) in 1838. There was dramatic expansion in east-coast transport and Aberdeen reaped the benefits. New tracks were constructed in and around Aberdeen and fine station houses were built by the B & O (1887) and the PW & B (1890).

Driving around the city, it is quite impossible not to know about the railroads. Like so many other American communities, the trains run right through or across the main streets! Although not accustomed to this, I soon regarded it as a totally acceptable part of the traffic. I really knew I was in America when I heard the unique wail of a train horn – it was a sound which I had heard in many a movie.

This Aberdeen experienced an even more remarkable growth after 1892, when it became an incorporated town. In a matter of years it had built its own fire station, telephone exchange and the First National Bank of Aberdeen. Aberdeen was well and truly on the 'fast track'!

In 1917, there was a boost to Harford County when the U.S. Government chose a site alongside Aberdeen as a facility to design and test ordnance material. Influential in the selection of the site were the excellent road and railroad systems which served the area. Aberdeen Proving Ground is a large military establishment, with its own ordnance museum which attracts many thousands of military enthusiasts and historians to the area.

From the north, I drove down Interstate Highway 40 across the mighty Susquhanna river and headed straight into town. Maryland has been a city since 1992, but retains a village atmosphere, quietly proud of its history and certain of its future as a high technology centre. I felt relaxed in the streets of this fine place, a hint of history ever present.

An air of grace and hospitality also exists here and its 13,500 citizens work hard at maintaining a caring community. This was recognised nationally in 1997 when Aberdeen was awarded the title of 'All America City'. An accolade which is not readily granted, it was awarded primarily for the efforts of the city to help its disadvantaged youngsters.

Downtown, I paid a visit to the Aberdeen Room, a local museum which successfully pieces together the unfolding story of Aberdeen. In the

First National Bank of Aberdeen cheque (1892)

museum I met with Charlotte Cronin, a charming lady, whose family came from Holland generations ago. Years of effort by Charlotte and Bill Cronin, and stalwarts like Ruth Duguid, have ensured that no detail of local history is left undiscovered. Indeed, it was at the museum that I found out that the sealed can in which we buy our beans is the invention of an ingenious local who sought a way to preserve fresh produce. Although slightly different today, the principle of the sealed, or 'leaded', tin can began here in Aberdeen, Maryland, and it started an industry which has served this community, the US Military and the rest of the world, extremely well.

Strolling around this green and spacious city, I was aware that the pace of life here has an easy rhythm. This is quite an achievement considering that Aberdeen is close to Baltimore, Philadelphia and Washington. I found this to be 'the Maryland way'. The tree-lined streets are bordered by stylish houses which whisper gently of earlier times.

Ernestine came here from Georgia and loves the place. As she said, 'It is a good place to bring up children.' You will not hear a better compliment than that!

The weather was becoming increasingly warm due to a tropical storm further south, and it became even warmer when I met up with city

Mrs Cronin tells the
Aberdeen story

Cal Ripken Jr., a true sporting legend

officials and staff. I had arrived late for an annual civic picnic, and let's just say that the delayed socialising was wholesome! The generosity of Mayor Wilson and the City Council, the ease with which the townsfolk approached a visitor, and the relaxed atmosphere of the place will entice me back. Next time, I will not be late for the picnic.

My few days spent meeting people like Darlene, Peter, the Cronins, Ruth and her sister Anna were special. It was a delight to be among such friendly and interesting people. Typical is the 'Italian Shoemaker', whose son had just clinched a contract to polish the boots of the military at the Proving Ground. In true Italian style, he is doing them by hand!

Sadly, there was not sufficient time to learn all of Aberdeen's remarkable history or about those whose efforts have contributed to its reputation. But I did hear of some great sporting heroes, none more successful than the Ripken family. Cal Ripken Jr., one of America's top baseball legends, is rightly celebrated in the Ripken Museum, where he is recognised for his outstanding achievements and his unique sporting lineage.

The location of Aberdeen is in a pleasant part of Maryland and though it was easy to find, it was hard to leave. It lies close to the natural beauties of the vast waters of Chesapeake Bay, which attracts outdoor sportsmen and lovers of all types of water sports. As a result, it is no surprise to discover that this area is one of the most popular holiday locations on the east coast.

However, lying as it does between the flat Tidewater area and the rolling hills of the Piedmont Plateau, Aberdeen offers more than natural assets and a great location. It provides an insight into the history of America's east coast. Maryland was one of the original Thirteen Colonies, first settled in 1634 and becoming a state in 1788. Aberdeen has every reason to be proud of its role in the development of the Old Line State.

To linger here would have been a real pleasure. However, I had to move on, taking with me recollections of a grace and style which is not normally sensed in a community of this size. This, truly, is a beautiful city.

I can still see the fine avenues of trees, the historic homes, feel the cool breeze wafting off Chesapeake Bay and hear the laughter after the picnic. I have to return, if only to know how the 'boot polishing' enterprise is doing. Ahead, a short drive north would take me to the State of Pennsylvania and two lost Aberdeens.

Would I find them?

Aberdeen, Pennsylvania, U.S.A.

Two Aberdeens, a Mill and a Dyke

Pennsylvania has the look of a model landscape with model farms and animals scattered here and there. Elizabethtown, Lancaster County, was the destination from where I would look for a very small Aberdeen.

Beth Wood Stiner, at the Chamber of Commerce, directed me down a wooded road towards an old mill. There I saw the sign 'Aberdeen Mills'. The mill, no longer in use, looked as if it had been uplifted from Bavaria. The old stone buildings are pointed and decorated in a style which is most definitely not American.

There is a reason. Pennsylvania was settled originally by Quakers and others who had fled religious persecution. In this State there are families from Germany, Russia, Scotland, England and elsewhere in Europe. Many of the farms that I drove past were owned by Amish people, their small black buggies trotting through the fields with purpose and along the highways, with risk.

The old Aberdeen Mills near Elizabethtown

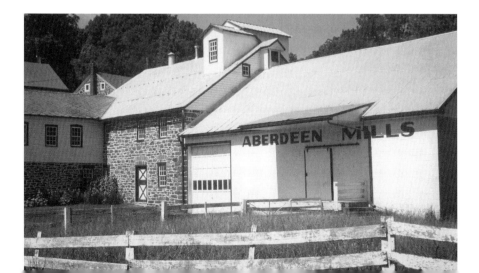

Aberdeen Mills, which had once supplied flour to neighbouring townships, had been built in 1774 by a German couple, Ulrich and Barbara Scher. The mills were situated alongside the Pennsylvania & Philadelphia Railroad, which connected Lebanon to Cornwall. Even a pleasant time with the family who now live in the old mill house, revealed little of how the mills acquired their distinctive name.

Further north, in Lackawanna County, I had heard there was another Aberdeen. This one was even more difficult to find than the one in the south.

Just beyond Scranton is a small town named 'Moscow'. From there, a road runs through quite stunning farmland and is called 'Aberdeen Road'.

It seems that around 1824 Richard Edwards and his family left Scotland to settle and farm in what is now Madison Township. There are old farmhouses scattered around and some of the barns look as if they store a memory or two! Little is known about the Edwards family, who have gone from these parts, but they left me with convincing evidence of their Scottish roots. In wandering around this charming location, so reminiscent of a warm July day in rural Aberdeenshire, I spotted a 'drystane dyke'. For those unfamiliar with that Scots terminology, it is a stone wall built by skilfully laying one stone on top of another. No mortar or cement is used to bind the wall. It holds together because the stones have been carefully laid to fit each space and their collective weight holds them in place. This is a technique used all over Scotland wherever there is stony ground – in the north-east of Scotland, that means just about most places!

Seeing this dyke in Pennsylvania convinced me that a farming family from Scotland had been around, and it is probable that the Edwards family had brought their skills to this rural area. I cannot blame them for settling here in the Keystone State. The soil is productive, the sky and land easy on the eye, and for a moment or two I could hear the hint of a north-east voice coming from one of the old wooden barns.

I was far from Scotland now, but another Scotland was waiting to be visited, as I turned north to Canada.

ABERDEEN, CAPE BRETON, CANADA

An Earl, a Spa and Marconi

The indigenous Mi'kmaq, a branch of the Algonquin-speaking people have lived on Cape Breton Island for many thousands of years. This northern part of Nova Scotia is only one of the regions that the hunting and fishing Algonquins inhabited on the east coast of Canada. Their language lives on in place names such as Mabou and Whycocomagh.

Cape Breton, a British colony in 1629, was taken by the French, ceded back to Britain in 1763 and joined Nova Scotia in the new self-governing Dominion of Canada in 1841.

Channel Island families arrived in the late 1700s and the Irish came from Wexford and Cavan, after the Irish Uprising of 1798. They were followed by Lowland Scots. Some of them arrived as disbanded British military people, others came as miners in the 1800s. Highland Gaels came in search of new opportunities and many English families fled here from America during and after the War of Independence. In the late 1800s, Italians, Jews, Scots, Ukrainians and Afro-Americans arrived to work in the steel plants. A truly incredible mix of people! Place names like Inverness, Dunvegan, Mull, St Esprit, Judique and Bras d'Or show the origins of these early settlers.

As I drove north from Halifax, I felt that I really was in another Scotland. The landscape was familiar, with the distinct look of the beautiful West Coast of Scotland. I can now understand why so many Scots chose this place as a new home.

And of course there is Aberdeen. Not just one, but two! There is Aberdeen and New Aberdeen.

ABERDEEN, INVERNESS COUNTY, CANADA

Lake-side Charm

On the banks of the vast Bras d'Or Lakes, Aberdeen was originally called 'North Side, Whycocomagh Bay'.

People from Tiree, North Uist, Lewis, Harris and Skye settled here around 1820. All were Presbyterian in the early years, and church services were conducted in the predominant Gaelic. The first arrivals were the MacDonalds followed by the Mathesons, MacKays, MacRaes, MacLeods, MacLeans, MacFadyens, MacPhersons, Frasers, Carmichaels, Fergusons and the Logans. A truly Scottish community.

Mostly farmers, these folks lived on 100 or 200 acres, growing their own food, raising cattle and utilising local timber for their needs. They farmed the land and fished the Bras d'Or Lakes, some constructing boats for the fishing or building small schooners to ferry passengers across the vast waters to other communities. The lakes are partially salt-water and there was a plentiful supply of fish, a fair proportion of which was salted and dried in readiness for harsh winters.

For many years, the community of North Side (as it was then) had its own one-room school, until a larger consolidated schoolhouse was constructed in the 1970s. There was a house-based post office from 1899 to 1968, reflecting a time of prosperity and a national need to increase mail delivery to outlying areas. Rural delivery was boosted by the new Trans-Canada Highway which makes its way alongside Whycocomagh Bay. The highway also brings in regular traffic and the bonus of summer visitors.

As to the name, it is thought that in the 1890s the Earl of Aberdeen, Scotland, and his wife stayed in a hotel in Whycocomagh which was run by the Mitchell family. They were probably 'taking the waters' at nearby Salt Mt. – a health spa popularised in Victorian times which still offers restorative hope. 'Whycocomagh', the name given to this area, means 'Head of the Waters' in the language of the indigenous Mi'kmaq. It is believed that the town was renamed 'Aberdeen' to mark the noble visit to North Side.

The entire Cape Breton region provides constant reminders of a powerful Scottish heritage. Early in July a festival is held here which features Gaelic concerts, dances and sporting events. Nearby is Baddeck, home of the Alexander Graham Bell National Historic Park, and testament to the impact of this Scots-born inventor. They are but a few reminders that thousands of Scots settled here and, listening to the local people, I distinctly heard a soft Highland accent.

Today, there are around seventy homes in Aberdeen, some one third of which are summer houses. Homes hug the water's edge, protected by birch, beech, maple, pine and spruce, which tumble from the steep hills to the lakeside. The population of around one hundred and twenty work at either the gypsum quarry at Little Narrows or at the pulp mill in Port Hawkesbury. Some, like Allan Matheson, still live on the land first settled by his Scottish forebears in the 1800s.

However, forced exile does not come without heartache and difficulty. In those early years, the only available land to live on was the shoreline. The mountains were wooded down to the water's edge and Allan Matheson told me of how those first settlers had to sleep under upturned boats. It would be some months before they cleared back the forest and established a properly built community. These were tough people!

The waters of the lake are crystal clear and on the breathless day of my visit, the white St Andrew's Church was reflected as if in a mirror. Rarely have I experienced such clarity of air; this is a magical place.

I had heard that Mabou was only a few miles away and, since it is legendary for its live music, a brief visit was soon arranged. Breaking out on the west side of the island was breathtaking – it was the landscape of Wester Ross, Scotland, at its very best!

In Mabou, the birthplace of the famous Rankin Family (folk singers and fiddle musicians), my destination was the Red Shoe. It is here that the finest Cape Breton music is performed most evenings. Aaron McDonald did not disappoint that evening, nor did anyone present, as we stomped and clapped our way past midnight! I attend many a ceilidh back home in Scotland, but this was special.

The following morning a car journey through pine-covered coastal scenery took me north to Sydney and another Aberdeen.

New Aberdeen, Glace Bay, Canada

Gateway to Newfoundland

The bustling ferry port of Sydney links Cape Breton to Newfoundland. A short distance from the harbour, the road winds down the east coast of the island to Glace Bay, where there is a small collection of miner's houses. There are immense quantities of coal under the water and many mining communities were dotted along this part of the coastline.

New Aberdeen was one of these settlements. The mine (No. 2) opened in the late 1890s and it is probable that miners from around Whycocomagh settled in Glace Bay. A row of miner's houses in New Aberdeen remains standing, enjoying a superb view out to the Atlantic Ocean.

Old miners shops and houses located at the magnificent Mining Museum capture the hardship which these families endured. It is also possible to venture underground and see the working conditions of the

Cool northern light at Glace Bay

St Andrew's Church, Whycocomagh

Table Head, the site of Marconi's transatlantic transmission

You can get
almost anything
here at Margie's,
New Aberdeen

Beneath the Saltire
on Lake Whycocomagh

Sparkling waters at Aberdeen, Whycocomagh Bay

time. These dark and narrow working spaces are many metres below the ocean. I have immense respect for all who toiled here.

Nearby is the world-famous site of the first transatlantic communication. In 1902, Marconi stayed here, sending and receiving telegraph signals at an installation at Table Head. The original transmission equipment can still be studied at the heritage museum – a fascinating place.

Although not possessing any local government, the folks of New Aberdeen are clear about its identifiable 'sense of place' and former residents are fiercely proud of their village. Today, New Aberdeen is somewhat in decline, although there is work at the steel plant in Sydney or seasonally at the inshore fishery and fish processing plant.

It was moving to be in this far northern Aberdeen, on a coastline not unlike our own north-east. There can be fewer places in the world where Scottish traditions and the Gaelic language have survived with such vigour. In Scotland, we have deep admiration for the way in which so much of our heritage lives on here. It is said that per square mile and per head of population, Cape Breton has more fiddlers than anywhere in the world. We Scots owe a huge debt to Cape Breton. It is a storehouse of our music, language and culture.

Looking south to the prairies and the next Aberdeen, I took with me many memories of this beautiful location. Friendly exchanges in Alice's Restaurant, the beauties of Lake Ainslie, the sea inlets, invigorating light and air, and a most fascinating description of eagles from a smiling Mi'kmaq Indian. As he told me, Cape Breton supports the largest concentration of Bald Eagles in north-east North America.

The name of my Mi'kmaq acquaintance? James Angus! What else could it be in this most Scottish of overseas locations?

ABERDEEN, SASKATCHEWAN, CANADA

Wheat, Ploughshares and Fraserburgh

In one of Western Canada's best wheat-growing provinces, almost twenty miles north-east of Saskatoon, lies the township of Aberdeen, a community of around six hundred. This particular Aberdeen is very aware of the struggle against searing hot summers and ferocious winters to establish a life in the Canadian prairies. It is in its written history.

Some who came here were immigrant farmers looking for better soil and an opportunity to work their own land. Others were settlers attracted to the promise of a new life in Canada. The first families set up home at the end of the nineteenth century and Aberdeen was incorporated as a village in 1907.

Provincial regulations demanded that settlements needed a minimum of 'fifteen occupied dwelling houses' and the arrival of European immigrants, Mennonites from Manitoba and others from eastern Canada and America ensured that this requirement was met.

With land superbly suited to growing wheat, the area around Aberdeen was soon very productive. Connection to the grain transportation system via the Canadian North Railway confirmed the township as an extremely

Isaac Bergen and Corny Boschman's 'Stanley Jones' harvester

Jacob Lane's barn
is almost there!

successful agricultural centre. In 1908, one hundred and twenty cars of
'hard wheat' were shipped out of Aberdeen. For a small community, that
was an incredible amount of wheat, as Henderson's *Western Canada
Gazetteer & Directory, 1908*, records:

> A population of three hundred, a daily mail service and elevator capacity of
> one hundred and twenty bushels, four general stores, a lumber yard, three
> hardware stores, a furniture store, a butcher shop, two livery stables, a
> blacksmith, a harness maker, an implement dealer, a bank and a hotel.

Such was its reputation that, in 1910, Aberdeen was described as 'a town
that does things'.

I met up with Ed Decker and his wife, Marlene, at the airport in
Saskatoon and we drove to Aberdeen. Although it was dark, I was aware of
a sky which seemed to go on for ever and ever.

Next morning, I looked round a compact and well laid out township.
Dominating the skyline were huge silos, from which millions of bushels of
wheat are poured into freight trains bound for all corners of Canada and,
ultimately, the world. The cereals which we eat may well come from around
here.

I stayed with Malcolm and Ingrid Weir on their farm and their kindness gave new meaning to the word hospitality. Malcolm's parents came here from Scotland in the early 1900s and we toasted them with a dram of Scotland's favourite beverage! In common with many others who settled here, Malcolm's mother and father put in years of solid, hard graft to establish a life and to contribute to this township.

The people of Aberdeen, Saskatchewan, come from hardy stock and in 1982 to celebrate seventy-five years' history, the Aberdeen Historical Society published a book recording the growth of the community, not in the usual terms of grand achievement, but by description of each family. It is a fascinating record of early life in the Canadian prairies. A comprehensive account, it tells of hardship, determination and a remarkable collective will to maintain sound community values.

Dugald Mackay and his family

Many families pulled together to make this Aberdeen. In recalling Isaak E. Bergen, born in the Ukraine, 1870; 'Blacksmith Bill', born in Southern Russia, 1894; Benjamin Wruck, born in Poland, 1865; Dugald Mackay, born on Islay, Scotland, in 1874; Frank Epp, born in the Ukraine, 1869; and Elliot Gordon, born in Tweed, Ontario, 1869, we catch a glimpse of the town's mixed cultural origins.

'Here to entertain you!' The Bergheim Band of 1918

The influx of Scots and others from Europe was enhanced by the arrival of the Ukrainians around 1898 and the Mennonite people in 1901. Their religions, languages and customs have made Aberdeen a fascinating and multi-cultural community.

The first school was Aberdeen School, 1908, followed by many others serving the needs of the various people. The catchment area was wide, taking in youngsters from outlying farms and lunch breaks were extended to allow pupils time to feed their horses. The names of these students would grace a United Nations agenda – Regush, Deptuck, Phaneuf, Weir, Reimer, Hamm, Dyck, Friesen, Quiring, Buhler, Mackay and Cruickshank.

Aberdeen grew from those names.

Among the first to arrive were the Scottish brothers, Dugald and Sandy Mackay from the Isle of Islay, accompanied by John Mowatt from Fraserburgh, Scotland. They worked hard through the winter of 1903, showing typical prairie endurance and fortitude. It is claimed that after a day's work, the Mackays would walk all the way to Saskatoon to have their plough shares sharpened, returning to start ploughing again next morning. Dugald was renowned for his ability to bake bread and he and his brother Sandy enjoyed as hard a social life as they did a working one. Especially with their friends, John Mowatt and Peter Dyck.

A well-attended Mennonite Sunday School picnic

A local businessman, Peter enjoyed the company of the Scots and it is claimed that he named the township at the suggestion of John Mowatt from Fraserburgh.

However, the story of Aberdeen does not belong to any single family or to one nationality. Others from Sweden, Poland, Russia, Germany, the Ukraine and elsewhere put down roots in this part of the world. They worked, sacrificed and gave so much to the history of the Canadian Prairies.

Strolling along to Gordie's Bar to meet Ed, I commented to Malcolm about the prairie sky in this vast, flat landscape. He told me of the farmer whose dog ran away. He then claimed that the farmer stood on a chair and watched it for three days! The humour is as dry as the summer. As for Gordie's . . . how does Buffalo Burger and Saskatoon Berry Pie sound? It tasted absolutely delicious.

More food, this time a 'pot luck' dinner, gave me an insight into the genuine warmth and closeness of these Aberdeen folk. Brenda, Bea, Ed, Malcolm and the others ensured a wonderful evening, but the night was capped when an attractive Mountie, referring to her splendid red dress uniform, paid me the compliment by saying, 'It is worn on very special occasions, so that makes you special.' I did not argue with this bonny lass!

Aberdeen has slowed down a bit, an inevitable result of commercial and industrial growth in neighbouring Saskatoon. This is often the way with a small community, lying close to a large city. However, this prairie town is an example of what can be achieved when people of diverse backgrounds join together in a common purpose.

Aberdeen is now one big family. That is the prairie way.

BON ACCORD, ALBERTA, CANADA

A Mill, River and School District

The province of Alberta invites superlatives, containing visual gems, such as the Columbian Ice fields, the Rockies, rolling prairies, emerald lakes and white-water rivers.

In this beautiful location lies the town of Bon Accord; its story begins in 1878 when a mill settlement was established on the southern bank of the Sturgeon River. Hunter gatherers like the Metis shared the land around Bon Accord with fur trappers who were mostly French or French Canadian. The new mill, built by the French Oblates of the St Albert Catholic Mission, was to transform the lives of those who lived in the area.

St Christopher's Mill, as it was called, included a grist mill operated by water wheel and a water-turbine-driven sawmill, which ensured both good flour and an ample supply of prepared lumber. By 1880, the mill settlement

Another Aberdeen which has pride in its flowers

included several houses, a chapel, the mills and shelter for livestock. The land beyond and around St Christopher's Mill was surveyed by David Beatty of Ontario in 1882. It was described by him as having 'fallen and burnt timber, poplar, willow, dense brush and several sloughs'.

Sadly, in 1889, a devastating fire destroyed most of the mill, but this rich farming region continued to attract more settlers, most of whom built homesteads close to the old mill. By 1892, the community had grown and the New Lunnon School and post office provided a base for the increasing population which was spreading along the riverbanks.

Among the earliest to settle here was Richard Cunliffe. By 1895, Richard had an established farm with seven residents. He and his farm-worker, Karl Neilson, were determined to make a success of the farm and between June 1895 and August 1896 they had '38 acres cleared and broken, 50 acres fenced, 6 acres planted in crops, a 75-foot well dug and cribbed'. They also built a stable, hay shed, hog pen, poultry house, shack and granaries. They constructed a house with shingle roof and a windmill to pump water, crush grain and saw lumber. It seems that they intended to stay!

Others, like the family of Keith Everett arrived and homes began to spread on both sides of the Sturgeon River. With some of the children having to cross the river to the only school, the daily journey at times became very hazardous. The solution was to create a school district on the north side.

A meeting was convened at the home of Alexander Florence in 1896 and a new school district was born. Florence named the new district 'Bon Accord', the motto of his native city of Aberdeen, Scotland. Historians still doubt the alleged origin of this motto. It is claimed that when the English occupied the castle of Aberdeen in 1307, during the Scottish Wars of Independence, the citizens put the garrison to the sword. To ensure that they knew who was friend and who was foe, their password was 'Bon Accord'. How interesting that such a motto is the name of this friendly community in Alberta.

The post office opened in 1901, the general store in 1903 and the school district grew rapidly. Bon Accord was firmly on the map; but not for long. When the Alberta and Great Waterways Railway built a line which came in from St Albert, the railroad company organised a new town, laying the plans for streets and commercial development. The only problem was that the site was one mile east of Bon Accord.

'Let's move,' was Bon Accord's reply.

When they face problems in Alberta, they are not afraid of making the tough decision.

In no time, Bon Accord had a rail station, post office, grain elevators, bank, community hall, church, houses and a general store. During the next fifty years it became one of the most friendly and well organised small communities on the river. In 1964, Bon Accord was incorporated as a village and by 1979 it had achieved the status of a town. Today, Bon Accord has a population around 1,500, which is quite a growth from the original seven on Richard Cunliffe's farm!

Driving the short distance to it from Edmonton, the neat Town Square with its clock, surrounding shops and shaded bar smiled at me from its warm midday slumber. In the bar I met Dave Latta, Mayor of Bon Accord. An invite to stay with Dave and his wife, Ann, was gratefully accepted, and little did I know what a stroke of luck that was. Dave carries an astounding knowledge of the town and its history. From him I learned of the new wealth in Alberta, namely oil.

The Town Clock in the square, 'where folks meet'

That answered my query about the countless contraptions which I had seen nodding their heads off in the surrounding fields. Dave called them 'pump jacks', and it seems that the rich, black soil is not only productive for crops, but has vast reservoirs of gas and oil below the surface. Walking over to a pump jack, the soles of my shoes quickly built up an inch or two of sticky black 'gumbo'.

Bon Accord is set in relatively flat prairie land and the fields which surround it are Canadian in size – this means vast, by most European standards! As ever in the prairies, there is clear evidence of the arrival of immigrants from Europe. Ukrainian churches are scattered around, and the locals say that the Ukraine people are the best farmers and make the best home-produced food. A typical neighbourly comment.

Dave had another surprise waiting – breakfast at Lily Lake. In a tranquil setting, the magnificent lakeside resort has facilities which attract corporation executives and companies from all parts of North America. Local people fish and canoe, surrounded by rolling grain fields of sweet yellow canola and carpets of blue flax. Breakfast was exotic and, had I been a visiting prince, I could not have been treated to more luxury. If you are fortunate enough to find yourself here, I would advise that you go easy on the menu – I was able to over-indulge with the excuse that I was doing so 'in the line of duty'!

Had I made the right decision to include Bon Accord in the list of Aberdeens? Most definitely. The hospitality of Dave and Ann was reason enough for any traveller and they embody the name of their town – the motto of my birthplace. If any doubt about their link to Aberdeen existed, it was quickly dispelled when I discovered that in Dave Latta's office there is a photograph of our Union Terrace Gardens and H. M. Theatre.

Being so close to the spectacular city of Edmonton and on the main route to Alberta's oil fields, Bon Accord is becoming a popular satellite town for business people. Poised on the brink of expansion, it has exciting years ahead.

It is fair to say that Bon Accord has found a new home and is well pleased.

ABERDEEN, MONTANA, U.S.A.

A Tornado, the Gills and a Box

Hot? Let me tell you about hot. On arrival in Billings in late afternoon, the air was blistering, the atmosphere sticky and the sky beginning to darken. Then it began. The most awesome electrical storm I have ever seen.

Lightning crackled on all sides and the air was charged with the smell of electricity. The cloud base lowered with the temperature and a cone-shaped mass wormed its way out of the greyness and pointed its narrow end to the ground. Could it be? Yes it was!

Taking the hint from other fleeing cars, I found myself huddled in a group of vehicles behind the solid wall of a gas station. Fortunately, the tornado, as it turned out to be, swept past less than one mile away. Within an hour the monster had gone, taking its monsoon with it. The evening then settled down to a display of Nature which crackled through to the early hours.

Next day, the temperature climbed steadily towards one hundred degrees and I set off on the long drive south to the Big Horn Mountains. Aberdeen, Montana, was my goal and my research confirmed that it lay just south of Wyola and only a few miles from the Wyoming State line. Easy. However, a surprise waited ahead.

No one local seemed to know of this isolated Aberdeen! I relied on my research and pressed on in that determined Scots way, and at last my efforts were rewarded. At the roadside, a sign clearly indicated 'Aberdeen. No Services'. However, not only were there no services, there was no township!

All that stood at the railroad line was a large shiny metal box, with a sign above it which read 'West Aberdeen'.

I needed to know more. By sheer chance, a rail-car made its way down the line and Gary, a railroad engineer, told me about this deserted Aberdeen.

Cheap
accommodation
at the Little Bighorn

It seems that a family called Gill came from Scotland to breed cattle at the edge of the Bozeman Trail, here at Buffalo Creek. The historic old trail led many a prospector across the blue sagebrush of Montana, the Treasure State. Alongside the trail, the Gills had one of the largest cattle ranches in southern Montana, with stockyards, corrals and bunkhouses. By the early 1900s, however, they had moved away, and the railroad eventually came through this stretch of the old stagecoach route.

Yet the name Aberdeen remains and the box is one of a number of switching boxes which allows the railroad to control traffic from as far away as Fort Worth, Texas. This Aberdeen may be the world's smallest, but it is certainly one of the most technologically advanced!

I returned to Billings by way of the site at Little Bighorn where General Custer and the 7th Cavalry were defeated. Among those who died at the Little Bighorn was John Stuart Stuart Forbes, the second youngest brother of Sir William Forbes of Pitsligo and Monymusk, Aberdeenshire, Scotland. Aged 27, he fought in the 7th Cavalry (Gray Horse Company) and is commemorated by a plaque in St John's Episcopal Church, Edinburgh, Scotland. A young man of north-east descent, so far from home.

From the battlefield, high on a hill, I looked west to the Snake River and my next destination.

The route of many a gold prospector

No stopping at this Aberdeen in Montana!

Sun-dappled Aberdeen, Idaho

Sprinklers water the dry Snake River Basin

ABERDEEN, IDAHO, U.S.A.

An Aquifer, Schools and Potatoes

For many centuries the land of the Shoshone-Bannock, south-east Idaho has been spectacularly known as 'The West'. In the early 1800s, hunting expeditions ventured into the valley of the Snake River, a region abundant in deer, elk and moose. One such group was the Astor Hunt party which passed close to where Aberdeen is today. Coincidentally, the Astors own Tillypronie House, less than two miles from where I live in Aberdeenshire, Scotland. Around 1836 it is recorded that 'Mrs Spaulding and Mrs Whitburn forded the Snake River on their mules' just above what was to be the location of Aberdeen.

Once opened up, pioneers moved into the region in 1860 – some in search of gold and the Oregon Trail, others seeking rich farmland and friendly community spirit. Both of which were to be found in abundance.

My own journey of almost three hundred miles from Boise rolled across the vast floor of the Snake River Basin, a huge natural flatland encircled with dramatic mountains and long-running escarpments. This is a true Western landscape. The heat was merciless and rose to 115 degrees that day.

Settlement of the area was encouraged by the Carey Act (US Congress, 1894). This allowed settlers the rights to take water from the Snake River and, by April 1906, Aberdeen was open for development. The Mennonites with their Dutch, German and Russian heritage, along with the Presbyterians and their Scots roots, came to work the land and build a new township.

I did not know how they arrived at the name for their new community, but I was about to be given a clue when I met Andrea Myler. She introduced me to Mrs Wryde, who explained more of Aberdeen's history.

It seems that a Mr Hamilton, from Scotland, was one of a group of early businessmen who formed a canal company. The canal is still visible and continues to irrigate nearby farming lands, and it seems highly probable that Mr Hamilton chose the name.

Aberdeen was incorporated as a village in April 1915 and became a city in 1941. Throughout its history there have been wonderful moments to recall. Helen L. Nichols remembers the hard years of the 1930s and the talk of a strange odour coming from a small local church. Further investigation in its basement revealed a large copper tank, lengths of tubing and curious valves and attachments. Apparently, the building welcomed prayers on Sunday and the production of 'moonshine' on weekdays!

Why not? This is a very dry region!

Helen also recalls the storage of ice, packed under sawdust, and so-called 'Rabbit Drives' when thousands of jack-rabbits were rounded up in a large wire-netting pen to be slaughtered and then handed over to local Indians from the reservation.

This small community in Idaho has had its share of characters, not least certain members of the Funk family. Peter Funk bought the old Wood Warehouse in the late 1920s. It had been a dance hall, theatre, roller skating rink and shooting gallery. Local folks anticipated him turning it back into one of these. But Peter had other uses in mind. He transformed it into a warehouse for storing sacked grain, mostly barley and oats. The sacks were piled to the rafters by hand. The most popular flour, Bannock Chief, was even stored in its own room and people traded grain for top-quality flours such as this.

Another member of the family, Alvin Funk, graduated in engineering and went on to plan and design the highway alignment through town towards Blackfoot. The same highway along which I had travelled from Boise.

However dramatic the scenes of my sweltering journey had been, they had been deceptive. Beneath this vast arid plain lies an abundance of fresh water trapped in porous rock. The mighty Snake River has created the world's largest aquifer and this vast underground reservoir is valued by all who live here.

The manner in which this part of Idaho utilises such a natural asset has to be seen to be believed. Typical is the farming community of Aberdeen, which makes ingenious use of its supply of underground water. All around are miles of sprinklers, watering thousands of acres of vegetable crops, under an endlessly burning sun. Yet the huge silos here do not hold wheat, as I had seen in Saskatchewan. This is potato country and the silos are vast storehouses of 'tatties'!

It is said that the best potatoes in the world are grown in Bingham County and that the best potatoes in Bingham County are grown in Aberdeen. This is no idle boast, since Aberdeen is home to the University of Idaho Agricultural Research Station. Research carried out here benefits the whole world.

Dr Sparks came from Colorado in 1947 and worked at the University of Idaho Research and Extension Center. His initial research was concerned with irrigation, vine removal, weather damage, harvesting, storage and handling of the potato crop. As a result of his work, Idaho potato processors and market shippers were able to operate for most of the year, despite the demanding winter climate. This became international news and Dr Walter Sparks gained world fame for his expertise on food management. His work revolutionised potato storage and is now standard universal practice.

'Trucks for Sale' – lots of them!

Aberdeen is a sleepy little town and walking around it there is little sign of its agricultural importance. This is one of the world's largest processing centres for the potato industry. Almost unseen, all manner of by-products from the annual crop make their way from here to every corner of the world. Next time you buy frozen chips, they may well have been grown and processed in Aberdeen, Idaho!

Farming, of course, has been vital to the area since pioneer days. Surrounding the new settlement were countless farming districts, each of which built a schoolhouse. Many of them also served as churches for the local pioneers. The schools and their histories tell the story of this region.

The earliest ones erected in the hinterland of Aberdeen were named Danielson Springs, Tilden and Otis – the door opening on Danielson Springs in 1890, the year in which Idaho became a state. Others followed, such as Springfield, Grandview, Sterling and Aberdeen.

Springfield School was a one-room building which was also used as a church for both Presbyterian and Latter Day Saints worship. Between 1912 and 1915 work was carried out to improve the amenity of Springfield School with the addition of 'coat and hat racks, coal bin gate, locks, bookshelves, hitching post and a new chimney'. By 1914, the trustees ordered the construction of a boy's closet, which was to be 'fastened to solid posts on the school ground, to prevent the wind and the boys at Halloween from upsetting it'. A wise precaution.

Grandview School opened in 1908, a splendid building with central heating and a modern gymnasium. The hand-painted stage curtain, which was decorated with adverts for local businesses, now hangs in the new Aberdeen High School.

In 1919, Sterling School had the luxury of indoor rest rooms and central steam heating. The youngsters boasted that the sub-zero Idaho winter could not keep them from their schoolhouse, since the basement was equipped with ladders, swings, sand and wonderful warmth. School was never so popular!

Fairview, Mt. Hope, McKinley, Williams, Mt. View, Central, Cedar Creek, Emms Dry Farm, Unical, Ringe and Yuma were but some of the numerous school districts within travelling distance of Aberdeen. In the 1940s all these small schools closed their doors and consolidated in the enlarging Aberdeen High School. Each one had served its own small rural community and Yuma School, which was a one-room log cabin near the

Snake River, was converted to a one-room building made of lava rock. It still stands proudly near the Will Harder Farm.

Inevitably, the schools had a tremendous influence on the area and I was told of a charming project, carried out in Aberdeen.

In 1988, the 4th Grade class of Mr Craig Wampler read the story 'Ernie and the Mile-long Muffler' by Marjorie Lewis. The curiosity of the youngsters was aroused. What would a mile-long muffler look like? The class began knitting and sewing, eventually enlisting the help of the whole school. With the support of Coats and Clark Co., who provided a thousand skeins of yarn, the mile-long muffler was completed in April 1989.

The author Marjorie Lewis came to Aberdeen to celebrate the achievement with a parade, speeches, television coverage and a community picnic. Truly an example of collective spirit and determination – the same qualities which the students' grandparents needed to establish this community.

The extremes from intense summer temperatures to sub-zero winters put frightening demands upon those brave souls, many of them Scots, who settled in southern Idaho. It took a special type of courage to move into these regions and it is a humbling thought to consider the hardships they endured.

On a very hot day in Aberdeen, I kept returning to the cool shade of the park at the centre of town. There I met a young lad, Beau, who almost tempted me on to the golf course. Too hot, Beau, too hot! But I will carry with me an image of the low evening sun shining through fine sprays of water, dancing from hundreds of sprinklers. Swaying rhythmically across acres of maturing crop, the sprinklers created a dazzling display of fairy-like rainbows.

'Potato is King' may well be the local motto, but there is so much more at which to wonder in the Gem State. This is a breathtaking region.

Here, at its southern end, are American Falls Reservoir and Pocatello in the Snake River Plain. Within a few hours drive are Yellowstone National Park and Jackson Hole, Wyoming. Twenty miles west of Aberdeen are the extinct volcanoes of the Craters of the Moon National Monument, a lava strewn and tormented landscape.

My stay in Aberdeen was all too brief – just I was becoming accustomed to the searing heat, the demands of my global journey pulled me back into the world of dates and flight schedules. However, the return drive to Boise

A typically warm welcome to Idaho

gave me an opportunity to divert to the Moon National Monument. I could scarcely believe the landscape which lay before me. Mile upon mile of grotesquely twisted lava outcrops led to the horizon and vast deposits of lava dust carpeted the soil in stark tribute to geological forces. Only two thousand years have passed since this ferocious eruption; this was a glimpse into the continuing creation of Idaho itself.

Astronauts, prior to going to the moon, came here in 1961 for on-site training, and among them was Alan Shepard, who was on the moon landing mission of 1971. Prehistoric caves, naturally formed craters and carbonated springs, can also be seen, with space and grandeur on a massive scale.

I was tempted to explore more of this magnificent State. My appreciation of the contrasts which are offered throughout North America was growing mile after mile. But another Aberdeen beckoned and I was about to meet a tree!

Driving in the USA

Once I had adjusted to being on the wrong side of the road and reading the overhead traffic signals, driving in America became a pleasure. Armed with Rand McNally's *Road Atlas of USA*, it is relatively easy to find a location and point yourself roughly in its direction.

Essential, is a companion who can share driving, read maps, anticipate turn-offs and stay awake when you are at the wheel, if only to keep you alert in temperatures unknown in Scotland.

Speeding is not a problem, and is minimised by keeping an eagle eye on all available mirrors for the Highway Patrol. Driving long distances in intense heat is dealt with by 'Air-conditioning'. In use, with all windows closed, you freeze to death. Switch it off, leave an arm hanging casually outside the car window for a few hours and you suffer UV burns to one arm only.

Take plenty water and snacks then plan ahead for stopping-places which can be sixty miles apart. Do not be tempted to stop at the roadside to ease bodily discomforts. There are snakes and sagebrush is very prickly!

Be economically aware if you need a mechanic. After stopping briefly in a small mid-west town for a two-minute tyre adjustment, I was asked for $25. I told the young lad that if ever he has a minor problem when driving through Logie Coldstone, our Jock at the garage will help him out for the price of a dram! Laughing, he accepted a few bucks for a beer.

Have a *Best Western* or *Super8* directory at hand and phone ahead to book overnight accommodation. If, on arrival, you find a local convention in town, be prepared to party with the crowd. There is no better way to meet a stranger and be counsel to his marital problems!

A drive of 6,703 miles took me around this vast country and, once the open highways are reached, there are few places in which it can be more fun to drive. Excellent roadside diners and low fuel costs kept this Aberdonian very happy.

Getting from one side of America to another when time is at a premium means flying. One of the 17 internal flights taken was from Seattle to Chicago – a mere 1,721 miles!

Unlike driving in the United States, being airborne does not allow opportunities to get to know the locals. There *are* no locals! Almost all my fellow passengers were 'company people'. Sitting beside a weary salesman with laptop churning out his monthly doughnut turnover does not encourage casual conversation, unless of course, you want to talk about doughnuts.

Youngsters heading for Lake Tahoe trying to stack skis in the overhead lockers, an exploding packet of pretzels which flew three rows in all directions and Alan cracking ankles with his heavy tripod provided most of the entertainment.

Many flights were from 'Hub' airports and a delay at Minneapolis resulted in a queue of planes lining up to take off at four-minute intervals. It was a bit like taking a bus to Mintlaw from Guild Street Bus Station back home except, in Scotland, waiting your turn means watching others head off to Stonehaven, Braemar or Alford!

I soon learned to arrive early, eat and drink before boarding (there are in-flight charges), have a good book handy, remain calm when explaining that Scotland is not in England and grab as much sleep as possible before the ensuing long drive. In 8,170 miles of flying I was impressed at the efficiency of America's internal flights, however, this is no way to see a country with so many stunning landscapes.

'Which way
now, Alan?'

Downtown
Aberdeen, Idaho

Hot and dry Snake River Valley

The 'Lady Washington' sets her sails

I meet a large tree!

Welcome rainfall in downtown Aberdeen, Washington

ABERDEEN, WASHINGTON, U.S.A.

Tall Ships, Canned Meat and Sawmills

The north-west coast of Washington, the Chinook State, was among the last areas of America settled by outsiders. The ancestors of the Quinault Indians first made contact with Spaniards in 1775 when the *Santiago* and the *Sonora* anchored off the coast and sent a party ashore to erect a cross and claim the land for Spain. The Quinault resisted this attempt to colonise their land and it took many years for trading trust to be established.

In 1787, six Boston entrepreneurs formed a partnership and purchased the *Columbia Redivia*, a fully rigged, two-decked vessel of 212 tons, mounting 10 guns. The *Redivia*, accompanied by the *Lady Washington*, a 90-ton sloop, sailed the inlets, trading otter pelts, which were bound for China in exchange for teas and silks. The Quinault Indians befriended Capt. Robert Gray, master of the *Lady Washington*, referring to him as 'a fair Boston man'.

On his second voyage in 1792, Capt. Gray entered a bay which he called 'Bullfinch Harbor'. Some months later, as master of the *Columbia*, he revisited the mouth of 'a great river' and named it in honour of his tall ship. Capt. Gray had named one of North America's greatest rivers, the mighty Columbia.

Sailing down from Canada, the English explorer, Capt. George Vancouver, visited the newly named Bullfinch Harbor and, in honour of Capt. Gray, he insisted that it be called 'Gray's Harbor'.

This coastline of numerous inlets and rivers, with a backdrop of soaring forests, had been home to native American Indians for thousands of years, but the arrival of white settlers ('Hoquates') was to alter their lives for ever.

The coastal indians were resourceful and strong. They were fishermen and hunters of game, seal and whale; they wove bark and reed, lived in split cedar homes and travelled the rivers and coastline in superbly crafted cedar

Gray's Harbor logo

and animal skin canoes. The abundance of food and shelter made these coastal people secure and wealthy. Their well-ordered lives allowed them time to create the most dramatic example of native art in all of North America, the towering totem poles.

This was the territory of many tribes. The Queets, Quinault, Chehalis, Willipa, Chinook and Quilente inhabited the coastline, while the Hoh, Humptulips, Ozette, Copalis-Oyehut, Shoalwater, Salish, Cowlitz and Satsop populated the rivers and to the north were the Makah. These tribes lived in a territory abundant with salmon, trout, tuna, bear, elk and deer. Indeed, the Quinault revere the salmon and one of their legends describes the vast numbers of this majestic fish and their special relationship with it.

A Quinault legend says that the Salmon People lived far to the west, beyond the ocean. The salmon species – coho, pink, chum, sockeye, chinook and steelhead – were the villages of the Salmon People. Only the Salmon People could decide if the salmon would run. To encourage the run, each Indian tribe took precautions, such as making sure their streams and rivers stayed clean. Many tribes held First Salmon ceremonies to honour the first returning salmon. The bones of the first salmon caught were carefully collected and placed on the riverbank so he could take his bones back with him to the home of the Salmon People.

The native Indians retain their fishing rights as a result of a treaty signed in the mid 1800s and use them with wisdom. Today, a number of tribes actively co-manage salmon resources with state and federal agencies. The return of salmon in the spring is still a cause for celebration. Many tribes still honour the event with a 'First Salmon Ceremony', recalling the distant history of the State of Washington.

The day I drove towards Aberdeen from Seattle it was raining heavily. The intense heat which I had endured in the Plains was a fading memory. I met with Angela Endres, a lively young lass who is responsible for welcoming visitors to her hometown.

We met at Billy's Bar, where the original owner had a reputation for dealing brutally with visiting seafarers. He plied them with drink and then allegedly dropped them through a hatch in the floor, where he stripped them of any valuable possessions which they might have had on their person. What he did with them after that is anybody's guess. Billy's Bar is now a very colourful and popular establishment and if ever you are in town, the Yakburgers served there are very filling and very tasty!

Angela enthused me with her tales and vivid description of the wonderful forests around here, in particular the Quinault Rain Forest. This is a vast recreation area which surrounds the glacier formed Quinault Lake. Angela's inviting picture of the Rain Forest tempted me and I was determined to see this unique area for myself.

Before that, however, I resolved to learn something more of the history of Aberdeen, and its many twists and turns.

'Now, that's what I call a timber-built bridge'

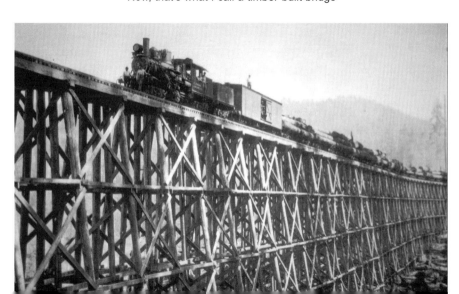

In 1825, a young scientist named David Douglas explored the region, studying the trees and plants around the Hoquiam and Wishkah rivers in particular. The size and beauty of the majestic firs so impressed him that to this day we call them 'Douglas Firs'.

In 1841, the Charles Wilkes expedition surveyed in Gray's Harbor country, establishing a white presence, and by 1847 William O'Leary was one of the first permanent residents in the area. Settlement was secured in 1868 when Samuel Benn traded his Melbourne property for 160 acres west of the Wishkah and immediately it was established as Gray's Harbor County.

At this time many miners were passing through the area, attracted by the prospect of fortune in Canada. Samuel Benn and his partners, Alexander Young and James B. Stewart, saw commercial possibilities in this passing trade. They established an enterprise which supplied canned butter and meat to prospectors. Stewart not only insisted that the works be called 'The Aberdeen Cannery', but went even further and persuaded Benn to

'Rafts' of big timber being towed to the sawmills

name the entire location 'Aberdeen' in remembrance of another place where 'two rivers meet' in his native Scotland. And so, Aberdeen, Washington, was named, then incorporated in 1889.

But is that the true origin of Aberdeen? Down in the State of Virginia, near Hampton City, there was an Aberdeen Academy for Boys, founded in the 1850s. One of its students, David Fleet, became an engineer and moved to Montesano, Washington Territory. On 15 November, 1883, he wrote this letter:

Montesano, Washington Territory

My own dear Mother,

I feel happier and more contented than I have for several years. Am glad that Will likes the gun and hope he bought in a good many sora with it. This is the greatest place for ducks and fish-salmon 6–25lbs: the best fish you ever ate. They are so plentiful, people spear them.

I think this will be great country in a few years. But for the weather and mud, this would be one of the most delightful climates I ever saw.

I have laid out a townsite about 14 miles below here which took about a week. Some said it was the nicest thing of the kind they had seen in this country. Those who have been here longer than 10 years are called 'moss-backs' because moss grows on everything in that length of time because of the rain. The butter and milk here are superior to any that I ever saw. I go to church ever Sunday and have been asked to lead the singing at the Congregational Church.

I hope to come home for a visit when I can afford it.

Best love to all.
Affectionately, David

Apparently, David Fleet named the town he laid out 'Aberdeen', after the academy he had attended in Virginia. Another letter of his, which is quoted in the *History of Aberdeen Gardens, Virginia* would also seem to confirm that this is the true story of how this Aberdeen got its name.

By the late 1800s the place was a successful, bustling frontier town and the harbour was becoming busier, since demand for lumber was growing at a phenomenal rate. Many sawmills were constructed and owned by A. J. West, the Wilson Bros., the Hulberts and J. M. Weatherwax.

The exciting growth in Aberdeen was mirrored across the river in Hoquiam. Both towns realised the need for a rail transport system if they were to expand and cope with a growing population and its needs. So the race began to complete the first rail links to outside markets!

Rail was salvaged from a wreck lying in the bay and rail ties made in the mill of A. J. West were donated to the effort. Even more amazing, town founder Samuel Benn offered 'a free lot of land to every man who gives ten days labor'. The Aberdeen 'management team' was determined to succeed and in 1895 the rail line was completed, four years ahead of Hoquiam! Aberdeen was now well established and generating wealth.

What of its location? There are many things which make this Aberdeen an attraction to visitors. One of the most compelling is the awesome Rain Forest. I was not prepared for the wonders of Quinault Rain Forest nor its timber. A short drive and I was soon among its dripping, moss-covered boulders. Giant ferns littered the forest floor and swathes of soaking vegetation draped a backcloth over towering trees.

Among all of this I met the world's largest Silver Spruce, a giant with surface roots as thick as most trunks. Can you envisage a tree one hundred and eighty feet high and ninety feet around? This is a primeval place where I expected animals from the Jurassic Period to appear from the mist!

However, a return to Aberdeen and a meeting with Al Waters at his home had been arranged. Al and his wife occupy the old Hulbert Mansion, a magnificent timber building. It had been the home of the Hulbert family, timber barons of their time. Timber was the making of Aberdeen and Al explained how a tragedy in California benefited Aberdeen.

At the end of the 19th century, the fire which destroyed San Francisco brought considerable trade to the timber barons of Aberdeen. Enormous quantities of timber were shipped from here to rebuild San Francisco. The birth of two cities at the same time!

In those boom years Aberdeen was a wealthy place and for more than a century the Jones family have been faithfully recording those times on film. Bill Jones, aged over seventy, is still working today and a visit to his photography studio revealed wonderful images from the city's history.

Washington State – big tree country!

Attention, 'wild rockers' out there! This small logging town is the birthplace of Kurt Cobain and his bass player Chris Novoselic. Their group, Nirvana, exploded on to the music scene in 1989, with most of the lyrics on their debut album *Bleach* about life in Aberdeen as seen through the eyes of restless young men. I wonder if they ever met up with Annie Lennox from my own Aberdeen?

Set in the Puget Sounds and surrounded by hemlock, spruce, Western Red Cedar and Douglas Fir, Aberdeen is an ideal location for those who sail, fish, hike and seek out Nature. Its population of around 17,000 enjoys a privileged setting in this corner of the north-west.

Aberdeen attracts countless visitors from Seattle and beyond. This is no surprise. This is 'big timber' country, the Evergreen State, and it merited more than my brief visit. If time had allowed, I too would have enjoyed exploring the surrounding vast wilderness.

With neighbouring Hoquiam and Cosmopolis, it shares a magnificent forest landscape and a coastline which offers outstanding opportunities to all who love to be near the drama of the Pacific Ocean. Here there is an opportunity to observe whales, tuna and all kinds of marine life, sights much as the coastal Indians enjoyed many centuries earlier.

The city is surrounded with countless natural treasures and I can understand north-east folks feeling at home in this majestic environment. It was, however, time for this particular Aberdonian to move on to a quieter fishing community in Kentucky, the Bluegrass State.

Aberdeen, Kentucky, U.S.A.

Ducks, the Devil and a Vagrant

Situated on the north side of the Green River opposite Morgantown, this was once a small coal-mining town. It is now a more tranquil community where folks come to hunt and fish.

In 1796, a man called Clark established a ferry and the township was born. In those days it was known as Clark's Ferry. The coal mine opened in 1800 and the coal was transported by barge to Bowling Green. River life was always precarious and within a few years the rising water washed out Clark's Ferry, putting a stop to the mining until 1896.

Around this time a Scots 'hobo' passed through the town, looked around and declared, 'You should call this place "Aberdeen".' And Aberdeen it has been since!

Two mining companies, the Reader Coal Company and the Phillips Coal Mining Company opened up new mines in 1890 and these were worked to exhaustion by 1906. During those years each company opened up a store and the community grew to 400 families. In those years the Old Aberdeen Hotel stood proudly, its massive log structure boasting a saloon, a drug store, twelve rooms and a porch running the full length of the building.

The hotel gone, all I saw was Aberdeen Store and a string of houses on each side of the road, with neatly kept gardens. The store reminded me of the old rural shops in Aberdeenshire, where you could buy just about everything. This Kentucky store was a combined coffee shop, greengrocer, newsagent, ironmonger, haberdashery, and bakery. I suspected that it was also the local community centre, marriage guidance council, citizen's advice bureau and group therapy meeting place!

Communities like this have endless tales to tell and I heard one of Jesse Haney Sr. who, at the age of 14, coming home in the dark from his work at the mine, thought he had heard the Devil. It was 1899 and Jesse approached a part of Aberdeen, then known as 'Log Town'. His only light was the faint glow which came from the oil lamp still on his head. He was brought to a halt by a bloodcurdling sound which filled the hollows and bounced from hill to hill. It seemed to come from the river.

Terrified, he ran for his life and was met by his mother, who cried out 'Bless the Lord, my boy is safe and sound!' Few mine workers ventured outside next morning for fear of a dreadful Satanic Judgement. By midday, however, the mystery had been solved. Apparently, one of the new freight and passenger steamboats on the river had just installed a 'wildcat' whistle and was showing it off to Aberdeen as it sailed past. There were a few sheepish grins about town that day!

The densely wooded hills rising from the Green River abound with wildlife and the river itself teems with catfish. This is a mecca for hunters and fishermen alike. I saw a sign in nearby Morgantown in which it claimed to be the home of the 'World Duck Shooting Championship'. I can believe it!

Time almost comes to a standstill in this secluded corner of Butler Co. Kentucky – the Bluegrass State. On leaving, I dropped in at the post office to have a laugh with Sue Morris at the way in which this Aberdeen acquired its name. Many Aberdeens were named by great entrepreneurs and founding fathers. This one was named by a passing vagrant! Little did I guess, however, as I leaned on the counter, how I would become such a vagrant during my travels in North Carolina!

Aberdeen's multi-purpose store!

ABERDEEN, WEST VIRGINIA, U.S.A.

A Church, a Graveyard and Memories

My destination in West Virginia was just south of Clarksburg where I had found an Aberdeen in Hacker's Creek. In a tight, twisting valley, heavily wooded and offering welcome shade from the sun, I came upon a group of local farmers who would surely know of the whereabouts of Aberdeen.

'No, never heard of it. Ain't no such place,' was the reply to my enquiry.

My research was put to the test and, being a stubborn Scot, I pressed on. Within a mile or so I saw the sign at the roadside, 'Aberdeen Cemetery'. Beside it stood a smart wooden house where three little girls played in the sunshine of the yard. Five minutes later and I was sitting with a cool home-made lemonade in my hand, hearing of Aberdeen from 'mom' Carolyn Hall. The lost community had been found.

Carolyn explained that it was normal around here to be wary of strangers so my farmer friends were giving nothing away. Was I a land speculator, or worse, from a local Tax Department? Now it made sense. Government officials are not warmly welcomed in Aberdeenshire, Scotland, either!

Sadly, Carolyn told me that the Aberdeen which I was seeking is no more. On the hill above her house is an old graveyard and a derelict wooden church. These are the last remnants of a farming community which died off as fewer young men returned from the World Wars. Scots, Irish and German farmers arrived here as far back as the 1720s and as well as their scattered farms, there had been a gristmill, barns, schoolhouse and church in this glorious spot, but now little remains of the small hamlet.

On a very hot day, I climbed to the top of the hill to see the old cemetery and church. On the way, I was wary of Carolyn's warning: 'Watch out for the snakes'. It seems that in West Virginia there are some pretty nasty ones, but my heavy breathing on the way up must have scared them off!

Carolyn Hall and her wee lassies

The old graveyard is overgrown. Hidden in the long grass, I could barely make out a few names on the stones. My findings confirmed the origins of the original settlers here in Lewis County. The folks resting here were called Hall, Lewis and Jamieson – good Scots names. Yew trees are sprinkled throughout the graveyard, reminders of an old Scottish superstition where they were thought to keep the devil away.

The derelict church was locked, but through the dusty windows I could make out the old pulpit and pews. The bell tower tilted from the roof and I envisaged it calling the faithful to Sunday prayer.

This well hidden location may not have fine avenues nor splendid buildings, but I found it extremely moving. It may have been the realisation that perhaps I was the first person from Aberdeen, Scotland, to have stood here for many years. From the hilltop, a valley of serene pastoral beauty spread beneath me. This area, known as Buckhannon, is in a quiet corner of the Mountain State but, at one time, north-east voices would have filled the air.

Aberdonians from Scotland once worshipped here

I was reluctant to leave this place, but glad that I had an opportunity to have a quiet word with fellow Scots who had travelled so far to settle here. A quick wave to Carolyn and her three lovely wee girls, and I was on my way again.

Aberdeen, West Virginia, is finally found!

These woods hide Appalachian secrets

Sleepy Arkansas front yard

'One day we'll fix the White River Ferry'

ABERDEEN, ARKANSAS, U.S.A.

Mystery, Buttons and Baptists

Almost fifty miles south-east of Little Rock, lies the hamlet of Aberdeen, Arkansas. Rolling terrain with a scattering of oak, hickory, elm and persimmon drew me along the black-top asphalt towards this peaceful and well hidden community.

In 1846, the United States of America sold 161 acres of land to Marcus B. Ragan. He gave 54 acres on the south bank of White River, Monroe County, for the building of a township. The town was laid out into twelve blocks and divided into lots of 100 feet by 140 feet. Streets were 80 feet wide and alleys 20 feet wide. From all accounts, the town had 'numerous buildings, with several stores, a large brick hotel, a livery stable, a Masonic Blue Lodge, a large sawmill and a large brick foundry, just south of town'. The township was called 'Aberdeen'.

In 1856, J. G. McGaughey, a Scot, received a delivery from New Orleans. It was the most complete assortment of goods which had ever been delivered to Aberdeen. 'Coffee, sugar, salt, whiskey, rice, fish, bacon, lard, molasses, candles, soaps, candies and sundries.' Aberdeen, Arkansas, was growing in size and style!

River traffic fed from White River into the mighty Mississippi and thence to Baton Rouge and New Orleans, some four hundred and fifty miles to the south. The township was a bustling and expanding community. It could not have anticipated how Destiny may have changed it for ever.

There is an uncertainty about events of 1862 and to this day historians cannot agree as to whether or not the town was destroyed during the Civil War. My research revealed information on this and I leave you to draw your own conclusions.

In his report of 9 July, 1862, Lieut. James W. Shirk, Commander of U. S. Gunboat *Lexington* stated:

At daylight we got under way again, and at 8.30 a.m. anchored off the town of Aberdeen.

On Sunday, the 6th. instant, Col. Fitch, went on a reconnaissance. At about 9 o'clock in the morning his advance of about 200 men of the 24th. Indiana Regiment, came up with and completely routed a body of the enemy's cavalry.

Despite stubborn resistance by Monroe's 6th. Arkansas Cavalry and the 27th. Arkansas Infantry, led by Col. James Shaker, Aberdeen succumbed and was all but completely destroyed.

Old buildings were demolished and the materials sold on for construction elsewhere.

It has been claimed that although no official record of Aberdeen's destruction exists, that may be because it was never owned by anyone, except by squatters rights. However, a document dated 1851 was unearthed which described the town layout and it was signed by Marcus Ragan and B. F. Eddins. Ownership, it is claimed, was based on the man 'who was the roughest, toughest and who shot the quickest'.

The historical accuracy of this account is open to debate. It could be that these events occurred some distance from Aberdeen. It is possible that the records reflect a falsified report. Then again, it could be true and the tale never filtered down to local residents. The truth remains a mystery. Whatever did or did not happen, those years impoverished many areas, such as the small communities of Arkansas.

In 1939, George Terrell left Stuttgart to find a place for hogs and for less than $12 bought ten of the original twelve blocks laid out for Aberdeen. George went to the State Land Office in Little Rock and, finding that no one, as yet, was paying taxes on the land, he became the owner of most of it until he sold up in 1954. The community of Aberdeen was, by now, firmly in the local administrative records.

What is indisputable is that the folks around here enjoy a life of great tranquillity on the banks of the White River. Steamboats with evocative names like the *Chickasaw*, the *Josie Harry* and *Hardcash* frequently came to the popular port-of-call. The *Chickasaw*, built by James Rees and Sons for 65,000 dollars, made her maiden voyage down White River on 28 November, 1883. She must have been a wondrous sight, since she was the first such vessel to have electric lights!

Aberdeen's peaceful First Baptist Church

That era has gone, but pausing in Aberdeen must have been a joy to river travellers. Where could there be a more pleasant location to moor your vessel?

Alta Bateman, writing in the *Munroe County Sun*, describes Munroe County as possessing 'An atmosphere heavy with the fragrance of wild honeysuckle entwined among the brambles; overshadowed by ancient oaks, persimmon and cedars which sheltered the homes of pioneers.' This was how I found Aberdeen, as I approached from nearby Roe.

It is a small community of scattered houses arched by trees, the eye caught only by the slight turn of a leaf or swift movement of inquisitive squirrels. The air has a sweet smell of persimmon and dried flowers, some of which were hanging from the decorated porches. I quickly understood that my relatively fast pace had to slow down. There is a rhythm here which is in harmony with its rural surroundings and such a location may best be served by a small community – Aberdeen has remained just that, tucked away in a beautiful corner of Arkansas.

Folk born here usually stay or return frequently to rekindle childhood memories. I met with Edna West, a charming lady who has corresponded with me for some years. In recalling her childhood of the 1930s, Edna describes the hardships of those years, as her father worked his twenty acres of land.

There was little employment and school was miles along a dirt road, in nearby Roe. Most work was found on the White River and youngsters like Edna would dig for freshwater mussels, steam them in a vat and select the best shells for the Button Factory in Clarendon. There, the shells were made into attractive 'Mother of Pearl' buttons, the fashion of those years. If Edna and her family were lucky, they might find a freshwater pearl in one or two of the shells. That was a great treasure!

Once a month, a vessel called *Fish Hawk* would come downstream carrying groceries and other goods to the small hamlet of Aberdeen. Edna recalls the joy of earning a small stick of candy as she helped her parents to carry the groceries some three miles back home.

Her father and her uncle ran a still, the whisky sold providing a much needed supplement to the family budget. She remembers being sent to keep a watchful eye on the road, just in case a car came along with a stranger at the wheel. A quick sprint into the woods would alert her dad and the still would be shut down! Times were hard, but they are recalled with great affection.

Edna has good friends in Aberdeen and I spent the afternoon talking with Mrs Dillard, Lara Weatherly and other local residents. They spoke of the closeness of the community.

The small white church at the roadside has played a significant role in binding these folks together. It too, has its story.

In 1958, Richard Cox, a counsellor and deacon of the First Baptist Church (Stuttgart) established Aberdeen Baptist Mission. On arrival from the Royal Ambassador Missionary Training Unit, Richard set about building a worthy church, complete with steeple. Throughout the next year many willing workers contributed to the task. The steeple was made in Cox's workshop, the green paint bought in Little Rock by the wife of Seth Hervey.

I met Seth and he reflected on those times. He spoke of how, throughout the work, spirits were upheld by a college girl who played a portable organ which she carried on each trip to Aberdeen. The organ was the size of an army footlocker and such devotion kept folks going.

As for how the place came by its name, that will have to remain a mystery. What is not a mystery is that this is an idyllic setting where 'rural

Edna West chuckles
at childhood memories

folks like to meet and eat'. In the midst of a demanding global voyage it was very tempting to consider spending some more time in this calming corner of Arkansas. A few days chewing the fat with the locals, catching some catfish and just soaking in the atmosphere seemed such a good idea. In Arkansas, the Natural State, this Aberdeen is content to set its own pace. Reluctantly, however, I had to pick up my own speed and head to the Carolinas, and an Aberdeen with strong Highland ties where I met a young woman with a longing to visit the Isle of Skye.

ABERDEEN, NORTH CAROLINA, U.S.A.

Scots, Timber and Turpentine

Once the hunting grounds of the Yadkin and Peedee, this area of dense pine forest was interlaced with Indian trails which were later used by European traders and trappers.

The story of Aberdeen, North Carolina, is one of three interlocked periods of history. These incorporate the establishment of the Bethesda Community, Blue's Crossing and Aberdeen itself.

BETHESDA

By 1745, the abundance of untouched land attracted many settlers to North Carolina's sprawling forests and fine, sandy soil. Highland Scots were among the first to arrive, with hardy men like Hector McNeill determined to make something of their new lives. Like so many, Hector had left behind the poverty and tragedy of an occupied nation, particularly the Highland region where the 'clan system' had been destroyed.

This period in Scotland's history is well documented, but interestingly the role of the 'tacksman' is often overlooked. The tacksman operated as a middleman between the clan chief and his tenant farmers, taking from the poor and befriending the rich and powerful. With the clan system gone, the tacksman found himself without a function. When forced sailings to North America began, this eighteenth-century opportunist was back in business! Possibly the original 'tour operator', he charged for passage to North America, paying a proportion to the landowners who wanted the glens de-populated. In turn, the landowners supplied an endless number of clients. As a result, some tacksmen arrived in America quite wealthy.

Not all Scots were forced to leave their country. Some were very enthusiastic at the prospect of a new life and new opportunities in a new land. It is possible that Governor Gabriel Johnston's offer of ten years' exemption from public and county taxation attracted more than the usual number of settlers, and very rapidly Moore County saw many Scots putting down roots.

In the 1700s North Carolina had America's highest concentration of Scots immigrants. Hector McNeill and others, such as John Patterson, James Ray and John Buchan, soon established a settlement at a beautiful area near Rockfish Creek, which they named 'Bethesda'. In 1767, Duncan and Margaret Campbell Blue arrived from Scotland with their son, Malcolm. They were to be influential in establishing a permanent community among the virgin pines.

Before returning to Scotland, Flora Macdonald lived for a time in the Carolinas. She settled there after a term of imprisonment in the Tower of London (punishment for assisting Prince Charles Edward Stuart to escape after his defeat at Culloden). It is very probable that she visited her fellow Highlanders at Bethesda.

In the manner of Highland Scots, these settlers wasted no time in seeing to their religious needs. Open-air services were conducted in Gaelic, drawing visiting Presbyterian ministers to Bethesda from other parishes in the Carolinas. By 1764 John Graham had established a school in order that

Burney's Store on South Street, 1925

A railroad town develops in the 1940s

religious and educational matters could be dealt with simultaneously, in true Scots tradition!

Tragically, in 1775 the American War of Independence thrust these new arrivals back into a period of conflict. Once again, Highland Scots were uncertain about their future and even more unsure of whether to be loyal to the British Crown or to their adopted land. For most, the choice was an easy one, since they had suffered at the hands of the British ruling class in Scotland and were determined to realise their dreams in this new land. No battles were fought near Bethesda community, yet many lives were sacrificed during the terrible struggle for independence.

By 1784, peace had returned, and energies could be directed towards a more productive future. Hector McNeill and his fellow Scots saw vigorous growth in the community, as grist-mills were built to convert corn to meal and saw-mills constructed to cope with the growing demand for lumber.

In 1799, the church at Bethesda found a home on Archibald Patterson's land and the ties of kinship, language and religious denomination forged a strong community, ensuring Bethesda's place in the history of North Carolina.

The Page Memorial United Methodist Church

Downtown Aberdeen, North Carolina

Tranquil Bethesda Church

Pinehurst's stylish Clubhouse

Arrival in Aberdeen from the north, took me down the highway to the edge of town. It would have been easy to miss the old downtown area, but my directions to this historic place were reliable. The short, but special stay in Aberdeen allowed me to meet up with some very wonderful people.

However, there is a way to go in the unfolding history of this community.

BLUE'S CROSSING

Malcolm Blue, whose surname is an anglicised version of *McGuirmean*, (the Gaelic for indigo blue) was one of the leading figures in the church at Bethesda and he transformed the region, laying the foundation for its economic growth.

An austere individual with immense ability to inspire, Malcolm owned vast tracts of productive agricultural land. He persisted in the conversion of the 'pine barrens' land into prosperous farmstead and by 1830 his many acres had become a successful enterprise. Twenty years later, he established the highly profitable production of turpentine, distilled from pine resin.

The Blue family made a remarkable contribution to the community,

The A. & R. Depot with engine all 'stoked up' for Fayetville

The Malcolm J. Blue Home, the first house built in Blue's Crossing

putting it firmly on the commercial map. The future seemed secure; but we know how capricious history can be.

The Civil War broke out in 1860 and had a devastating effect on those who lived in Moore County. Every family suffered the loss of brother, son, father or husband. The names of some of those lost recall the past – McIntosh, McLeod, McNeill, McMillan, McDonald, Patterson and Blue.

In 1865, a wing of General Sherman's army commanded by General Judson Kilpatrick camped at the Blue home. The next morning they narrowly escaped defeat at Monroe's Crossroads (now the Fort Bragg reservation). Part of the battle, known as 'Kilpatrick's Shirt-tail Skedaddle' took place on Battlefield Farm, owned by Malcolm Blue's brother, Neil.

After the war, the loss of five hundred men and the merciless burning of the pine forests devastated the region. Industrial recovery seemed impossible. But these were strong people in a very cohesive community and, with personal sacrifice and supreme effort, the folks of Moore County did recover.

As with all commercial progress, sound transportation follows close behind and in 1870 the Blue family brought in the Raleigh and Augusta Line to market their products of timber, tar and turpentine. The railroad crossed the old Peedee Road at an intersection which would later be called 'Blue's Crossing'; a deserved tribute to the efforts and contribution of the Blue family.

With a station and post office, Blue's Crossing was soon to become a major transportation halt, attracting powerful businessmen to Moore County. The east coast of America was becoming well populated and each expanding township required more housing. This was good news for the lumber industry, in particular for the many families who had settled in this area of vast pine forest. With the arrival of the Page family, Blue's Crossing was about to experience dynamic growth and undergo its final transformation to the name 'Aberdeen'.

ABERDEEN

Allison Page was a pioneer in the use of steam mills in lumber production and saw enormous potential in the pine forests around Blue's Crossing. He established a timber felling and production industry which progressed the economic strength of the region to a level that few could have anticipated. The Page family decided that Blue's Crossing should become Aberdeen. Some say it was suggested by John B. Graham who had taught in Aberdeen, Mississippi, others claim that it was named after nearby Aberdeen Creek. Whichever story is true, the name of my birthplace had finally reached the Carolinas.

As Aberdeen expanded, so did transport, as Allison Page brought in Aberdeen and West End Railroad in 1888. Soon after, in 1892, John Blue extended the Rockfish Railroad to Fayetteville, 'The Road of Personal Service'. So it was that these influential families created a major centre for the efficient production of lumber and turpentine.

Pine tree rosin being loaded for the turpentine distillery

Aberdeen and Rockfish Railroad Company pass, 1902

Unfortunately, the timber trade suffered a serious setback. With uncontrolled market demand, the pine forests were cut down at a pace overtaking natural timber regeneration. The result was devastating – the industry that had made Moore County began to die back!

As we saw with Aberdeen, Scotland, sometimes Destiny lends a hand and so it was in North Carolina. Researchers had discovered that the previously undervalued sandy soil was ideal for the growing of grapes, soft fruits, cotton and tobacco. After initial trials, many enterprises were established, and Aberdeen made yet another recovery. Today, North Carolina, the Tar Heel State, is still the largest tobacco producer in the USA and the use of timber is more carefully managed.

Aberdeen looks back on a challenging and, at times, demanding history; its three thousand inhabitants are fortunate that much remains of the contribution of previous generations. This may be the home of the Coca Cola Bottling Plant of 1913, and the *Pilot* and *Citizen News Record* newspapers, but it is more, much more – it is a store-house of North Carolina history.

I had the pleasure of meeting many of the residents who devote considerable energy to the preservation of this city's long history. Martha Swaringen, a lively character by any standards, devotes much of her time to greeting visitors to Malcolm Blue's home and farm buildings.

This is a charming heritage centre which has its own museum in the old barn. It is a treasure trove of valuable information, well stocked and bursting with 'discovery corners', from ground level to top floor. The farmhouse is restored, as are the outbuildings, and it was all too easy to transport myself back to the 1880s. Local schoolchildren and visitors come here to learn more of their heritage. Youngsters love to re-enact the life and times of the early settlers, and I saw a group dressed in period costume, feeling and experiencing their way towards a greater understanding of those early years.

The tireless Martha arranged for me to meet with the local Historic Society and I came across some of the town's characters in Aberdeen Cafe. Located in the centre of the old town alongside the rail track, which still takes produce to Fort Bragg, the cafe was a real retreat on a hot day. A cool iced tea was a welcome and refreshing beverage! Lloyd and Betsy have been running the cafe for a time and Betsy chatted away in a captivating Carolina accent about her ancestry in Skye. How she would dearly love to visit that beautiful island one day. I hope you make it, Betsy.

I was particularly pleased to meet Mark Cox who had been corresponding with me for some time. Like so many around here, he has a gentle affection for the past and will play his part in keeping alive the history of Aberdeen.

I met so many wonderful people at this enjoyable get-together. Among them was a lady who had attended the church at the Six Roads in Hilton, Aberdeen, Scotland; and a sprightly old gentleman who had been stationed in Aberdeen during World War II.

We all shared an evening of laughter and stories as we tucked in to a typical Southern meal around the friendly tables of the Aberdeen Cafe.

The long history of Aberdeen is superbly documented in a publication of the Malcolm Blue Historical Society, entitled *Aberdeen, North Carolina*. I had read this before my arrival and wanted to visit a very special place mentioned – Old Bethesda Church. The church was the focal point of the original settlement and its link to Scotland drew me to its doors.

Set in gentle pine-scented woodland, the serenity of the white-painted, old timber church, with its modest yet proud steeple, had a moving impact. From an inside window I could look out on to the Old Cemetery and read names like Buchan, McNeil, Bethune and Blue on the gravestones. The cemetery is also the resting place of Walter Hines Page, ambassador to Great Britain during World War I. Here in this peaceful, well cared for resting place, the roles of the Blue family and the Page family in the history of

Aberdeen are kept secure. I left Old Bethesda to its quiet calm and took with me a deep respect for the Scots who rested here.

Martha had arranged a meeting with Tony Robertson, Aberdeen's Town Manager, who spoke of plans to restore the downtown area to the elegance of its former years. As a member of Ballater Golf Club, my curiosity quickened when he admitted that one of the main attractions is the nearby Pinehurst Golf Resort.

Just out of town, the trees opened up to reveal golf course upon golf course – nine in all I think! Immaculately cut fairways, gleaming bunkers, glistening greens and empty tees tempted me, but I was only here to look. Buggies hummed their way from hole to hole and the golfers, in their shorts and straw hats, seemed to be having a great time. The clubhouse is striking and I walked in to the relaxed welcome which is so typically American.

I was hoping to meet up with Gordon McKinlay Jr., an assistant professional at Sandhills. His father is a golf professional in Troon where I spent many a year trying to master the 'impossible game'. It is still impossible! Unfortunately, Gordon was coaching and so our paths did not cross. Instead, I found time to browse in the pro' shop. It is bigger than our local supermarket!

On return to town I enjoyed a leisurely stroll around the old part of Aberdeen. With many thousands of miles ahead and frantic packing and unpacking between one location and another, it was good to slow down and savour the warmth and easy pace of North Carolina.

Early next morning, there was an incident which typifies the people of this Aberdeen. I had cracked a tooth on a cookie and required 'cosmetic dental treatment' for filming purposes. Ah, the vanity of would-be stars of the video screen! Mr Gant, a local dental surgeon, made the necessary repairs and when we spoke of his family roots, tracing them back to the Irvines of Drum Castle near my own home, all charges were waived. I think I was registered as a passing vagrant!

Back on my travels again, I left with rich memories of this Aberdeen, of the place, the people and the food – like the southern breakfast I had at Lee's place, The Inn at the Bryant House. Fresh fruit followed by warm ham sauce poured over home-made corn biscuits. Deeee-licious!

I would willingly return to the sweet smell of pine trees and the gentle ambience of North Carolina. Other visual delights, however, awaited me further south in cotton country.

ABERDEEN, MISSISSIPPI, U.S.A.

Steamboats, Cotton and Magnolia

On the west bank of the Tombigbee river, the city of Aberdeen offers true Mississippi elegance. The land on which the city now stands was once the territory of the mighty Chickasaw nation. A brave, noble and handsome people, they are honoured by Aberdeen as their land ancestors in taking their place upon the city shield.

After Aberdeen was settled, Chief Matubba lived in the township and Chief Hawambi lived nearby. The Chickasaw created numerous trails and it is alleged that along these passed Hernando De Soto, with his Spanish Conquistadors, in 1540. They must have been the first Europeans to set foot on the land which was to become Aberdeen some three hundred years later. De Soto also features on the city shield as testimony to the timeless settlement of this beautiful corner of east Mississippi.

Around 1831, Robert Gordon, a Scot from Dumfries-shire arrived in Cotton Gin Port to settle and pursue his skills as Indian trader, storekeeper, planter and land speculator. There is a strong connection between the name of Gordon and the north-east of Scotland. Huntly Castle, Aberdeenshire, is the ancestral home of Clan Gordon and, before the amalgamation of regiments, Aberdeen city had been home to the 'Gordon Highlanders' since their early origins.

Robert Gordon was present at the signing of 'The Chickasaw Indian Treaty' at Pontotoc in 1832 and was trusted by the Indians. He was granted a section of land for his part in the treaty signing and on this land he envisaged laying out a township.

Few places can claim to be called 'Aberdeen' by default, but apparently Robert Gordon did not like the way the locals pronounced its original name of Dundee, so he changed it to Aberdeen! And so, Aberdeen, Munroe County, Mississippi, came into being in 1835, when Halley's Comet would still have been visible in the night sky. Also featuring on the city shield, this heavenly sign seemed to herald good times.

Cotton was the main crop of north-east Mississippi and with it came immense wealth and a secure future for the town. So influential was Aberdeen in the cotton trade that its prices were quoted on the major world cotton markets. During the frenetic trading season, steamboats brought a variety of exotic foods, expensive furniture and other fine goods to the town.

In 1848, Aberdeen became the county seat of Monroe County and, by 1850, with a population of five thousand, it had grown to be a very wealthy town in a very wealthy county. The business sector prospered and merchants and plantation owners competed to build the finest and most magnificently furnished homes.

Many who came here were second or third generation Scots who had made fortunes in the tobacco fields of Virginia, Maryland or the Carolinas. It is worth noting here that Glasgow's late seventeenth-century wealth was largely due to the success of these 'tobacco barons'.

Stunning homes still stand here, their splendour open to visitors, and one of the delights of a visit to Aberdeen is the 'Search for the Gold'. This search is part of a tour of the city, during which it is possible to see more than fifty buildings in a range of architectural styles, spanning more than a century. From Antebellum and Victorian, to Greek Revival and Free Classic Queen Anne, there are cottages, mansions and ornate homes with stained and leaded glass, towers, brackets and bays. A veritable feast for the aesthetic eye.

The Orleana (1865), Sanders Place (1898), Steamboat (1899) and Shadowland (1863) are but some of the architectural gems which grace this Aberdeen. Each building possesses a unique charm, and they are all reminders of a different age. Most of the construction of these homes was done from the 1850s to the 1890s and timber is the main building material. Porticos are supported by elegant pillars, generous balconies command the view, and verandahs entice social gatherings out to enjoy the cool evenings.

House after house of quite stunning beauty – this was the astonishing sight which greeted me on driving into Aberdeen, Mississippi. The Main Street is mostly built in red brick, the sidewalks shaded by a canopy supported on elegant posts. Beyond the downtown area, tree-lined avenues hide magnificent mansions and numerous smart town houses. It is as if the

ABERDEEN

A

MISSISSIPPI
TREASURE

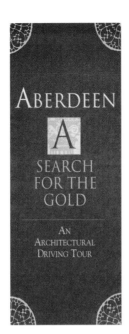

ABERDEEN

A

SEARCH
FOR THE
GOLD

AN
ARCHITECTURAL
DRIVING TOUR

Aberdeen, Mississippi, boasts outstanding examples of almost every period and style of Southern architecture. In this fascinating city can be seen three periods: Antebellum or Classical (1835–1865); Victorian (1860–1895) and Turn of the Century (1895–1920). It is this architectural richness which attracts many to visit Aberdeen and 'Search for the Gold'.

The wealth of cotton built this imposing home

The shaded
elegance of
'Greenleaves'

'The Orleana', a gentle and welcoming home, tragically destroyed by fire since my visit

'Sanders Place', a Southern gem

100% cotton!

A musical welcome to Aberdeen, Mississippi

Ferocious
High School
football
mascot . . .   . . . and
beautiful High
School Queen

Driving in the Deep South through Memphis

town houses attempt to echo the grandeur of the much larger mansions. Style and elegance abound in this community.

Special mention must be made of the outstanding Magnolias, a mansion in the ante-bellum style. Lush avenues of magnolia trees lead up to the house, its spacious front portico and double doors framed by multi-coloured stained-glass side lights. Susan Evans, Director of Tourism and enthusiast of the city's architecture, showed me around. Ascending the wide stairs to the porch and entering the large front door, did not prepare me for the dignified majesty of the interior. Inside, there are double parlours, once used for a tableau style wedding, and the exquisite tri-level mahogany stairway is a masterpiece as it meets and crosses in the hall, only to separate again before ascending to the second floor. The furniture, wall hangings, fine fittings and tasteful decoration spoke from a different age. The crystal oil lamp, grand piano, silver tray, rosewood table, elegant brass fireguard like a peacock's tail and tall marble fireplace were but a few signs that this was no ordinary home. Truly a magnificent building, it was gifted to the city by Clarence Day of Memphis in 1986.

Cotton created the sumptuous wealth, but Aberdeen's location was the most important reason for its role as the main centre for cotton export. Beyond Aberdeen, the river was not navigable for large vessels and all heavy traffic stopped here. The Tombigbee provided cheap and speedy transport to the cotton ports of New Orleans and Mobile. It was the highway down which cotton was shipped to the world, and up which came the fruitful return.

In little over a decade, Aberdeen became the second largest city in Mississippi, boasting the Gordon House Hotel and the magnificent Temple Opera House, the finest on the river! This was 'boom town'.

Tragically, a terrible event lay round the corner which was to have a devastating effect on Monroe County.

In the 1860s, the 'Civil War' or 'War between the States' exacted a heavy price; no family was spared tragedy or the loss of a loved one. Such sacrifice is quietly commemorated in Old Aberdeen Historical Cemetery, dated 1838. It contains both a Confederate section and an Old Fellow's Rest, where among many others lie a number of Scots. The most devastating carnage of the war is poignantly recalled at Shiloh, a few hours drive to the north.

On a warm Southern afternoon, I visited the old Cemetery and was moved by the rows of simple gravestones which recalled those who gave their lives. Many of the stones had Scots names on them. I still find it hard to grasp the fact that so many left our small country and gave so much to new causes. Grey serge for Confederate uniforms was woven in Aberdeen, Scotland. A sombre connection!

It took some years to recover from the conflict, but by the 1880s Aberdeen was soon on its feet once more. Transportation in and around Aberdeen was enhanced by the construction of three branch railroads, the Mobile and Ohio in 1869, the Illinois Central in 1883 and finally the Frisco 1886. Meanwhile, river traffic had resumed and soon a thriving whisky trade was developing. So successful was this trade and so widespread was Aberdeen's reputation, that it was known as 'Jug Town' for a brief and glorious time! But Mississippi 'went dry', and Monroe County voted liquor out in 1901. Jug Town instantly lost its attraction for many users of the river.

At first glance this is a quiet and elegant city, but civic life is very colourful. Each July and October the river is covered with decorated boats during the Blue Bluff River Festival. My visit co-incided with a fun parade through town, which combined the school Football Team Homecoming and the Cotton Exchange, a festival which celebrates the great years of the cotton trade. That night I listened to the authentic Southern sound of the 'Blues' and shared a barbecue supper under a huge yellow moon. It was entrancing.

The local journal, the *Aberdeen Examiner*, prints a special edition for these very special occasions. Clyde Wilson works at the *Examiner* and this charming Southerner is a fountain of knowledge of the history of Aberdeen. He gave me much of the information which I have recounted.

Today, local industries, such as timber, soya bean, chemical and cotton production provide a firm base to the economy. The Tombigbee also provides an attractive watersports facility – a huge boost to the tourism trade. Aberdeen's population has grown to around 7,000 and it is the legal, political, industrial and social centre of Monroe County.

This is a fine city, aware of its Scottish connection, as seen by the inclusion of the bagpipes on the city shield. Family names such as Gunn, Crawford, McFarlane, Forbus, McCracken and Gordon are still around here.

Memories? Rarely have I been in such a location which delights the eye. The pace of the place allows its ambience to bathe you and the people – Susan, Mayor Tindale, Cassandra, Clyde, Fred the Fire Captain and his colleagues, Jackie, who gave me a big hug because she 'Ain't never seen a Scotsman before', John at the hotel and many others – were a delight to meet. Their Southern 'Hi y'all', soothed my ears.

In 1969, one of its most famous musicians came to Aberdeen, Scotland. Chester Arthur Burnett, better known as 'Howlin' Wolf', appeared at the Cowdray Hall to the delight of all the Blues lovers in the north-east of Scotland. This 'King of the Blues' is still revered both here and in his Deep Southern home.

Yes, Mississippi, the Magnolia State, is proud of Aberdeen, which it rightly refers to as 'A Mississippi Treasure'. A return here is high on my list.

However, the distant High Sierra beckoned and the journey continues eastwards.

ABERDEEN, CALIFORNIA, U.S.A.

Sidewinders, Mules and Dance Nights

The valley floor between the High Sierra and the Inyo Mountains in this rugged part of California – the Golden State – is a popular route for visitors on their way south to Los Angeles, or north to Mammoth Ski Resort area.

In many ways, the valley has returned to the times of Joseph Walker, who led an expedition of fifty-two men through Owen's Valley in 1834. In those days it was an unknown wilderness sandwiched between the awesome Sierra Nevada and the Inyo Mountains, home to the Piute Indians. A peaceful, resourceful and socially sophisticated people, they accepted the passing through of white people. Little did they realise that the discovery of vast deposits of mineral wealth would unleash a dramatic change on their way of life. Between 1859 and 1900 events were to shake the valley to its very core! When silver was discovered at Comstock, to the north of the valley, prospectors, miners, mule-skinners, drifters and the usual entrepreneurs, flooded into Owen's Valley by the thousands.

This short and dramatic history of gold and silver fever in California has been well documented and it is beyond all doubt that the wealth generated in this region made California the great state that we know today. Vast mine dumps may still be seen at Cerro Gordo, once California's largest silver and lead producer. Remarkably, the deposits at Bodie, now a ghost town, produced gold valued at more than one hundred million dollars! At that time this represented the largest concentration of mined wealth in the world.

It is not easy to confirm how this impacted upon Aberdeen, which lies south at Goodale Creek, since little is recorded of it in those years, but no doubt it played its part in servicing those on their optimistic route north.

Aberdeen seemed to fare better, however, after the gold fever subsided in 1900. In the intervening years it had become a township with its own

The original Aberdeen Store. Built in 1921, it measured 30 x 20 feet

school, general store, gas station, post office and railroad halt. It is probable that folks who came to this area liked their new environment and stayed on. Hearing of the restoration of sanity to the valley, others came to join them and consequently, in the 1900s Aberdeen was known as the 'hub of the area'.

Being driven up from Los Angeles some three hundred miles south, I knew that I was entering a unique environment. To the east was Mojave Desert and much further north the infamous Death Valley. I was entering a landscape, the like of which I had never seen. My Californian friend, Peter Korngiebel, was driving and for the remainder of my time in Owen's Valley, he was an incredible host, guide and mentor.

As we approached the valley, a string of snow-covered mountains loomed to the west, among them Mt. Whitney, all of 14,300 feet high. To the east the Inyo Mountains ringed the horizon. Deeper into the valley, we were soon surrounded by a wall of majestic peaks on all sides. This is High Sierra country and somewhere at the foot of these giants is the small community of Aberdeen.

I was to hear of remarkable changes in the valley from Raymond Steffen, a handsome old gentleman who had spent his childhood in this wide, tinder-dry valley of sagebrush and coyotes. But it had not always been so, as he was poignantly to describe, sitting in the heat of his yard one late afternoon.

Raymond recalls arriving in 1915 with his parents, brothers and sisters –

his tale typical of the lives of families who came to the valley. The Steffens came from Los Angeles, bringing all that was needed to build a homestead: 'horses, cows, chickens, forge, anvil and tools of the trade of the blacksmith and millwright'. Their home was constructed from the ground up, the wells from the ground down! In time, with the skills of a responsible father and support of all the children, a secure house was built for Raymond and his family. They shared a lively community life with other arrivals in Owen's Valley. Each warm and dry homestead offered a welcome to all the neighbourhood.

Official recognition comes in 1980

12 INYO REGISTER–THURSDAY, OCTOBER 30, 1980

County plan now recognizes Aberdeen as a rural community

In its heyday, locals would come in their buggies from nearby Big Pine, Independence and outlying farms to socialise in Aberdeen with friends and family. Supplies were brought in by rail and Ray recalls the arrival of coffee in 25-pound cans; rice, oatmeal and cornmeal in 50-pound sacks; and large quantities of salt, beans, flour, sugar, bacon and salt pork, all from Ralph's in Los Angeles, a long way south.

Ray's hard working mother – 'one of the best cooks in the world' – kept the family going with home-made bread, biscuits and pies. When the hunting was successful, there was fresh duck and succulent rabbit stew. Fresh fruit and vegetables were purchased from local farmers to begin with, but the Steffen's deep wells would eventually irrigate 20 acres of alfalfa, corn, sudan grass, milo maize and corn flowers.

Self-sufficiency was essential in the valley. And the valley, from the Red

Raymond Steffen
recalls earlier years

Mountain Fruit Ranch to Aberdeen Store six miles south, was bountiful. Aberdeen Store was built in 1921, supplying gasoline, kerosene, motor oil and disolatate (later diesel fuel) to the local district and passing trade. The store sold general merchandise and was also a stage depot. The stage was an eight passenger Packard cloth top! For a time, the store was also the local post office and, at the age of seventeen, Ray's sister Irene was the youngest postmistress in the US. Aberdeen was also a base for a mule pack outfit; when visiting city folks came to hunt and explore the mountain trails, some would be taken by mule over the treacherous Taboose Pass.

Ray described his childhood years as 'a wondrous time when we all joined in and used what God had given us in the valley'. He enthralled me with his tales of those early years. Too many for me to recall, but he painted a vivid picture of a remarkable place.

However, one such story alarmed me somewhat. Apparently, he and eight-year-old Lucille had the race of their lives when they were pursued by a sidewinder snake. It was moving fast, but so were they, their wee legs driven by fear!

There was also the family trip to Los Angeles in the Model T. Ford. On the return journey, they got bogged down in Freeman Gulch and it took them three days to clean up the mud and debris, before making it home via Mojave and Olancha station.

Aberdeen School, close to the store, was the social centre of the valley; a place for 'pot luck' dinners, elections and church on Sundays. Les McAfee had the first radio and would take it to the schoolhouse so that all could hear it. A huge room was added where dances were held, attracting folks from as far away as Lone Pine and Bishop. Les played his harmonica with Henry Betancourt on steel guitar. When able to meet up, the four piece orchestra of saxophone, cornet, violin and drums, proved a great attraction. Men were charged a dollar admission and the women were free!

Leela Bell Howard recalls how, as children,

> They bedded us down around the big pot-bellied stove and danced from sun-down to sun-up. They had contests with prizes. One time my mom and dad, and Kate and Les McAfee sat around the table all evening before the dance with a great five-pound candy box. They dipped small rocks, cotton balls and tiny pieces of square wood in melted chocolate, to put in the prize box of candy.

She also records even more hilarious antics of her mother and father, and their crazy friends.

> They used to go up to the dances in Big Pine. One year they were going to a masquerade dance in the 'flivver' [an old Dodge car] with the men dressed as women and the women dressed as men. The men wore corsets, Les with his on upside down needing help from Kate to get it right. They set out on

The old schoolhouse of Raymond's childhood

Peter and Darlene's
desert home

'Hi, Jim. Tell
me about Laws
Railroad Museum.'

Weathered cliffs at the edge of the Mojave Desert

In the shelter
of the High
Sierra,
California

A very different landscape north of Los Angeles

Owen's Valley sketch

the Red Mountain Road and had a flat tyre. I can still hear Les saying, 'How in Hell can women do anything in these corsets?'

The dances held in the schoolhouse in Aberdeen are still remembered by the old-timers in the region.

The families who settled in Owen's Valley came from different countries, as reflected in names such as Nutgrass, Lutzow, Scalaris, Dewey, Cowsert, Armstrong, Smith, Ball, Migueron, Patten, Allen, Harvey, Orbin and Sigueron. Yes, this was a well populated valley of large ranches and farms with hayfields and flowing Artesian wells.

Thelma Mairs Cooper adds to the recollections of those pre-1930s days:

There were wonderful pit barbecues at the Calloway place across the river. In those days, the men sometimes shot game from the running boards of the cars as their wives drove. The women would fix it in huge dutch ovens, burying them in the sandy soil to cook. Everyone was welcome and contributed to the meal.

'All aboard' at Aberdeen Station

The valley may have set the standard for what we now recognise as true Californian ways! So what has happened to this lush and thriving region?

With an astonishing lack of concern for the folks of Owen's Valley, Los Angeles City eyed up the headwaters of Owen's River, filled in the wells on property which they had purchased, grabbed whatever land they could and effectively dried up the valley. All of this to supply Los Angeles with fresh water!

It began when Fred Eaton, ex-mayor of Los Angeles, started buying farms simply for their water rights. The city chose Rickey Farm as his headquarters, a ranch house of fifteen rooms, and it also bought barns and houses where people lived. Mr Eaton went on to buy a ranch south of Big

Pine and went into the chicken business while L.A. drained the valley. It is a long tale, but the result, sadly, is very apparent. In his lifetime of more than ninety years, Ray has seen a green valley with grass and orchards, turned into a dry desert overgrown with sagebrush.

To me, as a visitor, it all looked so dramatic, vast and spectacular.

I still had one question, however. Where did the name Aberdeen come from? No one knows, but it was the name the station adopted after its original name of 'Tibbets'. Tibbets Station was a water place and home for a section crew on the Carson & Colorado Railroad. After the Southern Pacific Railroad bought out the C & C, the name was changed to 'Aberdeen'. You can guarantee that a Scots railroad engineer had some part to play in that name selection!

Incidentally, the next station north was called 'Alvord' – sounds very like 'Alford' in Aberdeenshire to me.

When the gold dried up, many prospectors stayed on to work on the railroads and I would hazard a guess that some Scots were among those who gave up gold for steam! Perhaps they came from the old mine at the Black Rock Fish Hatchery which was close to the railroad station.

I visited the Laws Station Museum, just beyond Bishop, and heard more of the railroad from Jim Saylor, an enthusiast and guide at the museum. Jim lives and breathes railroad history and described how the Carson and Colorado Railroad constructed a narrow-gauge line from Carson City, Nevada, to a point over three hundred miles south at Keeler, California. His ginger beard glowed with pride as he showed me around the museum

Aberdeen Resort trailer-park lodge

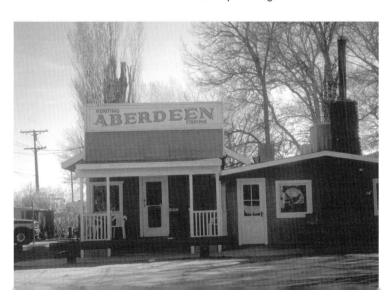

grounds. We paused at the station house, looked in at the Wells Fargo Office, and strode along the wooden platform as if we expected a train!

Jim has incredible knowledge of the history of the railroad and the years when it took passengers and goods across this dusty valley floor. In moments, he had me imagining the old trains huffing and puffing their way along the narrow gauge tracks. Today, visitors pass by on the new highway, but Laws Museum is endeavouring to roll back the years and plans are in place for a short length of working line, which will recreate the excitement of rail transport in Owen's Valley.

Jim, I hope your dream comes true.

My final visit was to the old store at Aberdeen, which Ray had told me so much about. Now it is the lodge of a resort area where visitors come to hunt, fish and mule pack up the foothills of Mt. Whitney. Some traditions live on, I'm pleased to say! Marty and Diane Fortney run the resort and they introduced me to some of the folks who stay all year round. Characters a-plenty here!

Close to the lodge, I visited the ruins of the old schoolhouse and imagined Ray and his brothers and sisters sitting there, gazing out at the clear blue sky reaching out to the distant snow-capped peaks of the High Sierra. How could they concentrate on lessons in a place like this?

My stay here was busy and fulfilling. Peter and his wife, Darlene, were very generous hosts and from them I learned much about Owen's Valley and its history. The days were hot and the nights were cool, under as clear a sky as anywhere on the planet. The images which surrounded me, will not be forgotten. Nor will the tales of what we carelessly describe as 'development and progress'. It can so coldly tear apart lives, as it did in Owen's Valley. Despite everything, the valley remains a place of breathtaking beauty. Stop off, should you be passing by. Perhaps, if you wander close to Aberdeen schoolhouse, you may even hear echoes of the music which rang out on Dance Night.

If visiting, take care not to bite down too hard on any chocolates you win in a prize!

ABERDEEN, FLORIDA, U.S.A.

Retirement, a Beach and a Forbes

Aberdeen, Florida, presented me both with a delightful opportunity and a firm refusal. Miami was the base from which I planned to visit Aberdeen, and here I met up with an old school friend, Isobel, who left Scotland many years ago and now lives in Miami. We shared valuable time recalling the highlights of a happy childhood in Woodside. As a bonus, Isobel's young sister, Margaret, who also moved to Florida, joined in our recollections. We have all lived busy lives and catching up was quite a task!

However, I had to leave Miami and travel three hundred miles north to Ormond Beach, to seek out another Aberdeen. Beyond Daytona, I approached my next discovery, on Highway 95. A sharp turn into Ormond Beach and Aberdeen was signposted.

Under a brilliant sky, the gates of this Aberdeen looked inviting, if surprising. An Adult Retirement Community and estate of more than four hundred homes, with a resident population heading towards 1,200, this Aberdeen is securely guarded. For many months I had attempted to make contact with various agencies in Ormond Beach. With no success, my visit was totally unannounced and consequently, the Security Officer at the gate refused me permission to enter. The owner, Donald Forbes, was away on business and no one was going to grant me access to the estate without his sanction. I respected the decision, but still managed to sneak a brief look at the splendid houses set amid rolling lawns. Every facility is here – meeting places, sports facilities and many other community amenities.

Then I headed for the beach. This is, after all, the Sunshine State! The magnificent Ormond Beach is only one part of the east coast of Florida, which rolls its many golden and sandy miles back down to Miami.

The long drive back south was hot and I admit to a certain sense of irritation with myself for not having succeeded in contacting the owner of

Sign up, folks, for luxury retirement

Aberdeen Retirement Community. Months later, I received a letter from Don Forbes and discovered the reason for the name. Don's family came from the Aberdeen area in Scotland, five generations previously. He chose the name and frequently returns to his roots in Scotland. Don, next time you are in Scotland get in touch and I will see what can be done to make sure Aberdeen is open to you that day!

Obviously, I was disappointed we did not meet up, but in a global voyage of this complexity, there is almost certain to be one or two hitches, and also bonuses. If I hadn't tried to visit this Aberdeen, I would never have met up with my childhood friend, Isobel. She wound up the visit to Florida by executing the most skilful high-speed drive through Miami to the airport so that a flight could be met. Eyes were shut as we flew through the traffic and the flight to Jamaica was saved by seconds!

ABERDEEN, JAMAICA

Sugar, Logwood and Invercauld

The history of Jamaica is complex and turbulent. There were many who sought to gain possession of this beautiful Caribbean island. The original Taimes, Arawak-speaking Amerindians, lived on the island some 1,500 years ago and called the place Xaymaca, meaning 'land of wood and water'. Christopher Columbus arrived in 1494, heralding the end of the culture of the Taime people and the island became a Spanish colony from 1509 to 1655. This jewel of the Spanish Main, which became an English colony in 1656, finally gained independence in 1962.

Each occupying culture has left its mark, adding to Jamaica's richness and I was excited about my visit to this historic island. Little did I know what wondrous surprises lay in store!

It began with the first meeting with Addia Miller of the National Tourist Board of Jamaica. She had arranged transport and a driver. This invaluable service, so generously offered, was gratefully accepted. A black, smiling face greeted me and a strong hand clasped my own with genuine welcome.

'I am Fred,' I said to my companion.

'And I am Wallace Thomson,' came the reply.

This was the first of many Scots names I came across on the island. Wallace was a fund of local knowledge and he knew all the drinking stops! We headed west out of Kingston bound for a town called Black River in the unspoilt parish of St Elizabeth.

Black River is a thriving and lively harbour town and our accommodation had been arranged at the Invercauld Great House – the name of which was yet another remarkable Scottish connection. Invercauld is the name of an estate just a few miles from my home in Scotland and in Braemar there is a hotel called the Invercauld Arms. Amazing! The Farquharson family, who own the Invercauld Estate in Scotland, once had

The magnificent Invercauld Great House and Hotel

banana and sugar plantations near Black River and they must have taken the name to Jamaica.

The hotel is a magnificent building in Jamaican 'Gingerbread' architecture: delicate fretwork decoration laced along the verandah and carved on all the exterior woodwork. It was here that I met Marianne, with a smile as warm as the day. She is from Aberdeen and I could not wait to see her small rural community, which lies inland in lush tropical farmland.

Around here, and all because of a remarkable tree, there was once a thriving and successful international industry. Prior to synthetic dyes, manufacturers discovered that dark blue colours could be obtained from the local logwood tree. The textile industries of Europe soon demanded large quantities of this natural dye. During the late 1800s, trade boomed in Black River, and in and around Aberdeen.

Property owners made fortunes, local boatmen and wood chippers earned very high wages and, in one year alone, 115,000 tons of logwood were shipped to the textile houses of Europe. Many of Aberdeen's young men would have worked in the logwood trade. It is interesting to note that in Aberdeen, Scotland, there is a Jamaica Street, said to be named after a sea captain who lived there and traded in the West Indies in the 1880s.

During our journey, Wallace found some logwood sawdust at the roadside, dark red and gritty. I took it back to the hotel and later, when I immersed it in hot water, the most glorious transformation took place. The water turned purple, then shifted towards a deep blue, very like the colour of denims. This was the magical process upon which an industry was founded.

As we neared Aberdeen, we entered an exotic landscape of logwood, breadfruit trees, banana palms, chicory and sugar cane. The further we went inland, the more dramatic the vegetation became. Not far from Aberdeen we drove under the 'Bamboo Avenue', a stretch of road which for a mile or two has a large canopy of bamboo meeting in a vast cathedral-like archway across the traffic. This is a stunning island.

Suddenly, we arrived at our destination and I was thrilled to find a sign which read, 'Aberdeen Post Office'. It was very hot and Wallace suggested some refreshment. It seemed a sensible way to start my exploration of the village and a cool beer or two later I found I had learned a lot more about the place.

Mrs Lorraine Taylor provided the welcome drinks and explained that there had been a banana plantation on a hilltop above Aberdeen owned by

Marianne is
delighted to meet
a Scottish Aberdonian

the Earle family. To my astonishment, she went further and suggested that the name may have been given to the village by the plantation manager. His name was Alexander Forbes – the same name as my grandfather!

But that was not all.

The number of Scots names around here was way beyond anything I could have anticipated. It seemed as if every second person was called McIntyre, Wilson, Thomson, McPherson, Bruce, Forbes or Farquharson. Apparently, Scottish landowners sent hundreds, if not thousands, of 'indentured slaves' to work on the plantations, and their blue eyes, red hair and freckles can be seen in successive generations.

One Jamaican of Scottish descent was George William Gordon, the son of a Scottish planter, Joseph Gordon, and a slave woman. Joseph kept his family at a small community in the St Andrew hills. Sadly, he refused any of his children by the slave woman to enter the 'great house'. At the age of ten, young George was sent to live with his god-father, James Daley, in

'Do I get change out of that?'

Black River. There, he received good schooling and later became a lawyer who championed black rights. A respected figure in Jamaican history and a National Hero, George Gordon was subsequently arrested and hanged.

He was one of many Jamaican Scots who played an important role in the struggle for the rights of slaves and the island's independence. He paid dearly for his brave commitment.

Countless Scots place names are testimony to that long relationship. Close to Aberdeen is Monymusk, Perth, Dundee and Kilmarnock. In Aberdeen itself, a sign points to Upper Aberdeen and alongside it is the name Ben Lomond! I could have been in Scotland, were it not for the scenery and the look of the village. Its wooden houses and handful of shops are brightly painted; the gardens exploding with plants profusely covered in red flowers and sheltered by trees hanging with tropical fruits.

Below the village is the school, and I walked down to meet the principal, Yvonne Daley. It is possible that Mrs Daley is related to James Daley of Black River, the god-father of George William Gordon. She told me of the new industry which has sprung up around Aberdeen. The tree which provided rich indigo dye now has a much sweeter purpose. Honey! Our old friend, Providence, has ensured that the logwood tree still provides for the parish of St Elizabeth and breathes life into this small valley. Today, the same trees bloom 'in clouds of gold, wearing haloes of bees'.

The commercial success of St Elizabeth Logwood Honey goes from strength to strength, and it is claimed to be the finest honey in the world. Having tasted some of the golden nectar, I heartily agree.

This is a peaceful community and it would have taken little persuasion to have convinced me to stay on. However, the demands of a global schedule beckoned once more. Reluctantly, I left the smiling faces of the children at the school, nodded my farewells to the young men chewing on fresh sugar cane, posted some cards at the Post Office and finally extricated Wallace from Mrs Taylor's bar! It was time to return to the coast.

In a Caribbean sunset, we left the lush valley and returned to Black River. Many traders in town also have Scottish surnames: next door to Forbes & Co. is the Scotia Jamaica Bank. In the Invercauld Great House, the owner, Claudette Rose, spoke of her affection for this corner of the island.

Black River is an interesting town, and retains some fine buildings from the eighteenth century. One of these is the church of St John's, a splendid building designed to carry four clock faces, although currently possessing only one. The other three, ordered from England around 1785, have still to be delivered. Time here does indeed move slowly!

As he showed me around the region called 'Jamaica's Breadbasket', Wallace took great delight in drawing my attention to the unique sights of his island home.

'Look at that' he would prompt, time after time.

I would find myself catching a glimpse of crocodiles in the mangroves of the river; roadside vendors with fresh fruit stacked in a rainbow of colour; lorries piled high with sugar cane, thundering along to Appleton's Rum Distillery; or smiling women at the roadside selling freshly caught shrimp. There was always a new surprise! More than once I sniffed the sweet scent of burnt candy coming from cane fields as they were burnt free of debris, prior to cutting.

This is an astonishingly exciting place. Wonderful, just wonderful. It still astounds me to think that so many Scots have been such a part of its long history. Even at the last moment, I heard of yet another Aberdeen in the Parish of St Ann, at the top of the island! However, this news came too late, just hours before the flight out of Kingston.

Soon, I would be leaving to resume the search for other Aberdeens. I regretted having to leave such a fascinating island, a place of endless surprise.

School's out!,
Aberdeen, Jamaica

Main Street at noon – time for a cool drink!

'And I am pleased to be in your Aberdeen'

A Buckleys
School welcome

Old sugar-crushing windmill, Betty's Hope, Antigua

St John's stallholder

Smiling comes easy in Antigua

ABERDEEN, ANTIGUA

Windmills, Hurricanes and Tourism

As I approached from the air, below me stretched a string of emerald jewels on a sea of startling turquoise. These are the Leeward Islands of which I had heard so much. Somewhere down there was my destination, Aberdeen, Antigua.

It had been the territory of the Arawaks and Caribs for more than ten thousand years and was never conquered by any European power. Even Columbus sailed by the island and from a distance named it after the church of Santa Maria de Antigua in Spain. The settlement of Europeans on this island dates back to the British Navy who saw it as an ideal location for overhauling and repairing ships. Their chosen site was eventually named English Harbour.

Admiral Horatio Nelson spent some of his early years here, arriving at the age of 26, in command of the frigate Boreas. By the time he left for England and an illustrious career, the island had become a secure haven for British vessels.

I began my search for Aberdeen with a visit to the capital St John's. It is a fine city, with imposing stone architecture and a distinctly Spanish looking cathedral. Once a sleepy town, it is now a hub of activity, especially when the cruise liners arrive!

As I strolled along the quayside I could scarcely believe the sheer scale of these ships. They tower above the tallest buildings in St John's, emptying thousands of visitors on to the island. Remarkably, it has little effect on the gentle atmosphere of Antigua – on the contrary, the island has a relaxed atmosphere, which allows you to explore at your own pace. Small and easy to get around, the island has dozens of inviting coves, white beaches and numerous small villages.

One of these is Buckleys and it was there that I headed to find Aberdeen.

A short drive through a landscape of palm trees, coffee groves and avenues of tropical vegetation, soon took me away from the coast into a valley surrounded by low hills. On one of the hills I found Buckleys, but no sign or mention of Aberdeen.

When I met Patricia Joseph, principal of Buckleys Elementary School, all was explained. Aberdeen is a part of Buckleys and lies halfway down the hill. Everyone knows that the name came from Scotland, but there is no record of who brought it here.

I looked around at the surrounding landscape. The houses spill down the hillside, their colourful gardens ablaze with red, orange and pink blossom. I was very fortunate to have a reason to visit this beautiful place. From the school on the hill, the valley spreads out to other low hills around the island. Down in the palm-fringed valley, I could see numerous allotments, where local people grow their own fruit, coffee and sugar. Beyond, in the distance, I noticed some large stone towers and was curious to explore these peculiar constructions.

On the advice of Patricia, I headed to Betty's Hope, where I found a clue to the Scots names on this island and an explanation for the towers. Built in 1674 by Sir Christopher Codrington, Betty's Hope was the site of one of the first full-scale plantations on Antigua. The tall towers were wind-driven mills. Antigua, like most islands, uses wind as an energy source; its windmills once powered huge cane-crushing machinery.

By 1705, most of Antigua was planted with sugarcane; 170 mills were dotted around the island, each grinding out 55 tons of sugar per year. At Betty's Hope, a small heritage museum tells of the hardship of the slaves who worked on the plantations. Among the recorded names of those who were transported here are Scots names, such as, Grant, Crosbie, Doig and McIntyre. Perhaps I had found a clue to the origin of the name Aberdeen. It is very likely that a plantation worker or manager, exiled and far from home, decided to pay tribute to his birthplace.

Antigua has long given up its sugar industry, but has not forgotten the toil and sacrifice of generations who lived and died on the plantations. The tall towers stand as silent tribute to these souls.

Back in Aberdeen, I was hot and thirsty. Perched on the hillside is 'Dan's Caribbean Bar', a focal point for the community. I decided to pay it a visit for some light refreshment, and a chance to meet up with some local people. Unfortunately, it was closed; a pity, since it looked a fun place to be. Perhaps

Aberdeen, Antigua, a hillside paradise

it was just as well, as I had a flight to catch the next morning! Still thirsty, I walked halfway down the hill to buy nuts and a cool drink at a store. The owner was delighted to hear of my travels and proudly confirmed that she lives in Aberdeen. This paradise island, with lemons, bananas, guavas, mangoes, oranges, sugar and coffee, also has its own Aberdonians. The thought delighted me.

In true tourist style, a lazy afternoon was spent swimming in the turquoise Caribbean and controlled 'toasting' on the gleaming white beach at the Sandpiper Reef Resort. This is the life of which I had often dreamed. Could I just linger here for a few more days, months or more? Perhaps my wife, Margaret, could sell our house and join me?

The immaculate beaches and sparkling waters, the charm of historic St Johns and the easy smiles of everyone I met certainly invited me to stay. However, the serious and responsible Scot in me dismissed such personal indulgence, and my mind returned to the task. Ahead lay a few more thousand miles and the discovery of more Aberdeens.

Have no doubt, the delights of this island paradise were tempting, but flight schedules were tight and the Southern Hemisphere awaited.

The global journey was not yet over.

Aberdeen, South Africa

Karoo, Ostriches and Braakefontein

The Karoo is an expansive area of semi-desert in Cape Province, South Africa, divided by the Swartbeg mountains. Here, in this apparently unforgiving landscape lies the small town of Aberdeen. Almost one hundred and fifty years old, it is a treasure house of Cape Province history.

First accounts date back to 1689, when an expedition led by Isaq Schrijver went inland to barter for cattle and sheep with the Inqua Hottentots. Subsequently, more expeditions were planned and the area visited became an established 'meeting place'. It was to become my meeting place with Jean Watermeyer, with whom I had been corresponding for some years.

A long, hot drive from Port Elizabeth took me north towards Aberdeen. This was my first visit to the African continent and I was amused to see the telegraph poles festooned with groups of chattering monkeys.

Driving had its own hazards. In a trailing dust cloud, I swerved frequently to avoid giant tortoises as they crawled across the road, like decorated coffee tables on the move! However, within two hours the vast raised plateau of the Karoo was in sight and ahead lay Aberdeen. I knew that I had found it when I spotted the soaring spire of the church, built by two Scots, Andrew Murray and Thomas Menzies Gray, and said to be the tallest in all of South Africa.

Around 1812, the Voortrekker leader Piet Retief travelled through the area as a merchant and by 1817 land was sold to Jan Vorster, who established a farm which he named 'Braakefontein'. From the original Afrikaans, this means 'salty fountain' or 'brackish water'.

Following the Boer War the British acquired this region and deeds to the land were signed by Lord Charles Somerset. Ownership was transferred but the name Braakefontein stayed on. In 1855, it was sold to the Dutch

Reformed Church and plots were auctioned off over a period of four days. Eventually, a township grew around the farm and retained the original name of Braakefontein until 1856. In that year, the name was changed to 'Aberdeen' by the Reverend Andrew Murray from Aberdeen, Scotland. Andrew Murray's church had its cornerstone laid in 1860, was later enlarged and finally completed in 1907. It was the soaring spire of this church which had beckoned to me across the Karoo.

In dry, burning heat I finally met up with my friend and correspondent, Jean Watermeyer. She generously invited me to stay at her farmhouse where I encountered ostriches for the first time in my life – not surprising since Aberdeen, South Africa, and ostriches have a long relationship.

The fine houses in this town grew out of the wealth of a fashion industry. When, in the 1920s, there was a demand for ostrich feathers from the world's fashion houses, many ostrich farmers and traders in this region made fortunes. Aberdeen boasts a wonderful collection of Eastern Cape, Flemish, Victorian and Dutch Cape architecture. The 'Feather Barons' and their love of extravagant housing has made Aberdeen an architectural conservation town.

Today, ostriches are still bred for their leather and feathers. John Watermeyer keeps a few and these quite incredibly large creatures refused to come over and greet me when I approached the mesh fence of their pen. Big they may be, but they were quite shy when it came to meeting a Scotsman. Reflecting on my travel-worn appearance, perhaps their behaviour was understandable!

The Karoo is carpeted with short, scrubby grass and is mostly used for grazing cattle and sheep. John and his son also breed Angora goats. These strange animals with curly wool came from Turkey and like it here! The Watermeyers' home is typical of Karoo farmhouses, with a shady verandah protected by poplar trees. The approach is an avenue of magnificent cactus plants, beyond which are large bushes with lethal-looking spikes. These thorn bushes certainly do not grow in Scotland, and they merit considerable respect.

Water is drawn up from wells driven by wind pumps and the Karoo valley reminded me of the dry Snake River Basin in Idaho. It appears to be a dry wasteland, but it is very deceptive. When the original Voortrekkers travelled north, they observed the animals and followed them to find drinking water. In the rugged beauty of the Karoo there is abundant underground water, the area around Aberdeen having once been a vast inland sea.

In far off mountain ranges, I could see the dramatic 'Sleeping Giant', a high mountain contour which looks like a giant figure at rest. On a more intimate scale, I examined the incredible craftsmanship of a weaver bird's nest. The skill and care taken to create such a strong but beautifully woven basket is astonishing. The area is also a mecca for fossil hunters.

It was time to visit the town with Jean, and my first impressions were of the centre of a European town. Around the attractive town square, many fine houses have the decorative woodwork and fine wrought iron balustrades reminiscent of parts of Holland. I was, of course, looking at Dutch Cape architecture, adapted from Holland to the climate of Africa. The metal roofs elegantly curve down over the edges of the main structure and are painted in light colours to reflect the searing heat of summer.

There is a timeless quality to this old town, in the centre of a vast South African plain. Jean took me to meet her dear friend, Mrs Tina McCardle. Little did I know that connections would turn out to be closer to home than I could have imagined. Tina came here some years ago from her native Scotland and her son still lives in Alford, Scotland, not thirty minutes' drive from my home. It is indeed a small world!

A light lunch had been arranged in the church hall and I looked forward to meeting South African Aberdonians. On entering the hall, I was intrigued by a large mural which encircled the room. It is a significant piece of work, with twenty large panels depicting biblical scenes. All created locally. In

'It's not far now, is it?'

Large, but very shy at meeting a Scotsman

1999 a local artist assisted a group of dedicated women to create the panels, using wool, leather, net and voile. Word has spread about this artwork and it attracts visitors from all parts of the world. Aberdeen is proud of it, and rightly so.

Over lunch I met with some fine people who were all keen to know about Aberdeen, Scotland. Some have strong connections to the 'old country'. Later, with time in hand, I studied more closely the lovely architecture in this Aberdeen.

Hotels, private homes and offices have a character which tells of a time of considerable wealth. Worthy of mention is the Magistrates Court and Post Office building, justifiably a declared National Monument. Apparently, it was designed and planned to be built in Grahamstown, but somehow the drawings ended up in Aberdeen. At Grahamstown's loss, this ornate building, with dragon gargoyles and decorative brickwork, was erected in Aberdeen.

Another gem is the original farmhouse 'Braakefontein' which retains much of its early structure. The front facade is unchanged; inside the floors are yellow wood, the ceilings Oregon pine. The store room and stables still have wooden floors and reed ceilings. This first house in Aberdeen, built in the East Cape style, is now called 'The Homestead', and looking at it conjured up images of the early Dutch settlers.

In the cool and welcome shade of the colonnade of the town's main market building, I gazed at the neat town square, the elegant palm trees and fine architecture. It was hard to believe that this stylish Aberdeen is in the heart of the Karoo, some hundreds of miles north of Port Elizabeth.

Had the time been available, I could have discovered much more about this historic Aberdeen. I could only manage a short visit to the small and well maintained museum where it was revealed that a certain Captain Oates was hospitalised here during the Boer War. The same Captain Oates who famously said, 'I'm going for a short walk. I may be away for some time.'

Reluctantly, it was time to leave and pack memories away. I said good-bye to John and Jean (who even took the time and trouble to wash travel soiled clothes), their family and all the others who had been so generous in their hospitality.

The drive back to Port Elizabeth lay ahead and, in the early morning darkness, I was advised to watch out for kudu. This is an antelope which has the dangerous habit of leaping from the long grass into the headlamps of oncoming vehicles. Sometimes fatal! A seriously large animal, the kudu is not one to take lightly.

A canny drive until daylight led down to the coast and Port Elizabeth. On the road south, the sight of early sunrise over red soil, sparse grassland, distant mountains and the approaching sea etched vivid images in my mind. I am beginning to understand the magnetism of an African landscape. Beautiful South Africa, I would have loved to have seen more of your delights, but I will not forget you. Aberdeen, in the Karoo, drew me here and allowed me to experience this quite unique location.

What other surprises did the Southern Hemisphere hold?

Dutch Cape architecture
in South Africa

Aberdeen's
soaring
church spire

Sun and shade

Looking over Aberdeen, New South Wales

The old Aberdeen Meatworks Stockyard

Aberdeen, N.S.W. Australia

Green Ants, Beef and Vineyards

The drive north from Sydney was along the 'old road' through McDonald's Valley, and a quiet arrival in Aberdeen belied the unforgettable time which lay ahead. Within minutes of meeting another of my correspondents, Val Snow, my traveller's baggage was deposited at Kay and Gerry's Aberdeen Motel. A few minutes more and a cool beer was in my hand as I 'joined the lads' in an Australian pub! This was the prelude to a wonderful time in this lovely valley.

The Hunter Valley, New South Wales, is an area of delightful beauty, dotted with eucalyptus, wilgas, kurrajongs and Cyprus pines. In August, 1824, Henry Dangar crossed the Hunter River, surveyed the upper Hunter region, noted the prospects for a successful rural estate and made this known to others. The lush grassland and moderate climate ensured that this was to be cattle country.

The area was originally called 'Moonbil', a name given by a local tribe of Aborigines who occupied a 'bora site' close to where Aberdeen now exists. The word 'Moonbil' means 'the place of little green ants'.

I was mindful of this and kept a watchful eye out for the little 'stingers' as I sat on the grass with Val one afternoon and heard more of the story of Aberdeen; and a long story it is.

In 1825, Thomas MacQueen was granted 10,000 acres in New South Wales by Governor Brisbane. His agent, Peter McIntyre, selected land in the Hunter Valley and the new rural estate was named 'Segenhoe', after MacQueen's birthplace. Segenhoe estate prospered and soon Australia's first horse-drawn flour mill was working here.

Thomas MacQueen settled at his estate in 1834 and in 1838 he obtained approval for the laying out of a new town at a ford in the Hunter River. At MacQueen's suggestion, the new town was named 'Aberdeen', in honour of

George-Hamilton Gordon, 4th Earl of Aberdeen, a close friend from MacQueen's days as a member of the British Parliament. The Earl of Aberdeen became Prime Minister of Britain in 1852 – it is always useful to be well connected!

It was not long before the Scots arrived. They settled here during the 1830s, naming many local spots in memory of their homeland. Here can be found an Aberfoyle, Strathearn, Edinglassie, Scone, Roxburgh, Glen Dhu and a Clydesdale – all names from Scotland. Peter McIntyre was typical of the Scottish settlers who came here. He had won awards for his excellence as a farmer at Tomcairn, Perthshire, Scotland, and in 1825, with about twenty men and their families, he arrived in New South Wales.

Many other Highland Scots came to this area, and names such as Campbell, Cameron, Burns, McFarlane, McIntosh, Mackay, Buchanan and Stewart are still to be found here. Among them was a young bride – Jane McIntosh, from Aberdeen, Scotland, who lived the remainder of her life in Aberdeen, New South Wales. From one end of the world to another, without a change of address!

Slowly, Aberdeen grew and by 1841 it was beginning to establish itself. In those days, it consisted of six houses, a mill, a store and the Segenhoe Inn. The inn was licensed and provided food, drink, shelter, as well as post office facilities for travellers on the Great Northern Road.

In 1863, Murdo Cameron Mackenzie, from Dingwall, Scotland, arrived. A tailor by trade, he soon had a flourishing business with a general store and importing company. In 1866, he built the only remaining row of shops

Segenhoe, the name of the original estate

from those times, and his entrepreneurial skills earned him the honour of becoming the first mayor of Aberdeen, New South Wales.

In 1870, the Great Northern Railway line reached Aberdeen. The result was the expansion of the town to several stores, two churches, a school and a police station. By 1889, the population had grown to one hundred and fifty, and Aberdeen Inn – 'a fine two storey building, brick built, with shingled roof and verandah on three sides' – was constructed by John Cundy. The story of Aberdeen had a gentle start, but a major development was to have a powerful impact on the community. Australia's largest meat exporting centre was about to be born.

In 1892, the Australian Chilling and Freezing Company delivered its first cargo of 13,000 sheep and lamb to London and by June 1892 more than half a million sheep had passed through the works, bound for the world's markets. The meat processing plant became even more successful with allied products from dairy herds like 'Thistle Butter', which was produced at Aberdeen Butter Factory. This was another economic success for the township.

By 1910 the Commercial Banking Company of Sydney opened a branch in Aberdeen and the population grew to seven hundred. Aberdeen was the place to be, such was its growth and economic security! The future looked bright . . . or so it seemed until I met up with Les Parsons, who revealed more of the town's history.

He had worked at Aberdeen Meat Factory and explained that, because of a decline in the trade and growth in overseas competition, this once powerful contributor to the success of the town has been closed for some years. It ran from 1892 to 1992 and was a real giant in the history of Australian export. Its loss is still deeply felt in this valley.

However, this is the Hunter Valley and the soil is abundantly productive. A new industry is blossoming around Aberdeen and we all benefit! When next you purchase Australian wine, there is a fair chance that it comes from here. There are numerous vineyards in the surrounding area, many acres covered with row upon row of grapes, maturing in the sun and nourished by occasional soft rainfall. One such vineyard is Birnam Wood, a name chosen from Shakespeare's play *Macbeth*. A Scottish connection again!

A sample of the oak-casked wine convinced me that Australian wine can compete with the best. I humbly regard myself as a bit of a connoisseur when it comes to wine and I put this claim to the test when I attended a party that evening in the Commercial Hotel. Val, her husband Dale and what seemed to be most of the town had turned up for a Scottish get-together to hear about the Aberdeens of the world. To set the mood, a pipe band from nearby Scone was playing with great skill and energy.

A few hours and wines later, the pipes were put to one side and the band sang a selection of Scottish ballads, some from the north-east. This wonderful night was rounded off by a rendering of 'The Northern Lights'. Here I was, so far away from Scotland, and yet I felt very much at home. It moved me to think that there really is a family of Aberdeens uniting across cultural and national divides.

Next morning, Les took me to Segenhoe Stud Farm. Breeding racing horses is a very successful industry in the valley. Mr Cochrane, the stallion manager, showed me around and I saw a few of the magnificent animals which produce some of the world's finest racehorses. Many are sold in Ireland and other parts of Europe.

On returning to town, I walked under the verandah of a shopping arcade, so typical of earlier Australian architecture. It made me think of the settlers who had made their home here in this tranquil and compact community which nestles alongside the banks of the Hunter River.

Just beyond the town is Glenbawn National Park and I was advised to pay it an early morning visit to catch a glimpse of the parakeets, gunnas, kookaburras and the ever-present kangaroos.

Val Snow and her boys reflect on our global family

My dawn visit introduced me to rural Australia at its very best. As the low mist evaporated in the morning sun, I realised that I was being studied inquisitively by dozens of kangaroos, each tilting their head to catch sight of a visiting Scotsman.

Glenbawn Park is a magnificent asset to Aberdeen, its many acres covered with Cyprus, iron-bark, wilga, paper-bark, eucalyptus and kurrajong trees. The early-morning call of the kookaburra, the gleaming white plumage of the parakeets and the occasional shy glance from a kangaroo made a very early rise well worth the effort. However, I had some folks to meet at lunch-time and so, reluctantly, I tip-toed out of this magical place.

Back in Aberdeen, I was greeted by dozens of local people and shared in an 'Oz Sizzle', a barbecue with its own unique Australian energy. Everyone, or so it seemed, wanted to know about my Aberdeen and about the journey around the world. An interview on local radio, conducted with a glass of beer in one hand and a gigantic sausage in a bun in another will stay with me as a recollection of a totally crazy but wonderful afternoon.

There were quieter times which linger in the mind. The contemplative conversation with Val and her two young lads, Mark and Brad, was one of

'Was I in Australia, or only dreaming?'

those moments. We sat in the shade of an old tree, near the banks of the Hunter River. The wind in the dry eucalyptus mingled with the chatter of cicada on a typical Aberdeen afternoon. I knew that I was far from home when I heard the unique laughing call of the kookaburra and breathed in the spicy perfume of dry leaf litter.

I still savour the atmosphere of this small community. Neatly kept gardens front the houses and languid trees cast dappled light on the verandahs, making the town easy on the eye. A pleasant rural environment which I will long remember. More than that, however, I will remember the people. There are those with strong memories of their parental link to Scotland (a remarkable link from one end of the world to another), those who long to visit their roots and those who were just delighted to meet with someone from Scotland. Their hospitality knew no limits.

This small town, the birthplace of the 'Blue Heeler', a unique breed of dog, is home to special folks who know how to extend a welcome and how to party Australian style! I can only imagine what it must be like in July, when Aberdeen has its Highland Games on National Tartan Day – that must really be something!

If visiting, just watch out for little green ants!

Aberdeen, Hong Kong, China

Tanka, a Tramway and Dragons

To the Chinese, Aberdeen is still *Hueng Kong Tsai*, or 'Little Hong Kong'. This region of South China has an ancient history which is incredible. Bronze-age rock carvings, and a recently discovered 5,000-year-old kiln on Lantau Island, tell of early habitation of these islands and coastal inlets.

The history of this corner of Asia is long and changing. Hong Kong became part of the great Chinese empire during the Han Dynasty some two thousand years ago. During the fourteenth century, the area was settled by the 'Five Great Clans' and these dominant families maintain a strong presence to this day.

We all know the present economic stature of Hong Kong, but this is not a recent development. The importance of this region was established many centuries ago. Imperial records show that troops were stationed at Hong Kong to guard the pearls which were harvested locally by Tanka divers. They were boat dwellers, soon joined by the Hoklos who established fishing villages and created salt ponds in order to preserve their catch for the market at Macau. The steady growth of small villages on the many inlets and islands included a settlement which much later became the community of Aberdeen.

The coastal region had become infamous for rebellion and piracy in the seventeenth century and in a decisive move the ruling Manchus evacuated the whole area. They allowed settlers to return only when the 'bad elements' were cleared out. Eventually, the Hakka, or 'guest' people, were permitted to settle, and they brought with them the skills of farming rice, pineapple, tea and incense.

However, it was not in the nature of the region to maintain stability for too long and the British moved into the area in the 1800s, using the deep, sheltered port of Hong Kong as a base for the booming trade in silk, tea, spices and opium. The result of this intrusion was the dreadful period of the Opium Wars.

China eventually ceded the island to the British in 1842 and the name Aberdeen was given to the newly acquired harbour town by the Earl of Aberdeen, who was Secretary of State for British Colonies in the 1840s. Territorial expansion by the British eventually led to their possession of the Kowloon Peninsula and Stonecutter's Island in 1860. Consequently, the New Territories were leased to the UK for ninety-nine years, as from 1898.

I had known of this Asian Aberdeen for many years and I could not wait to see it and experience its atmosphere. Little did I realise that Hong Kong would overwhelm me with its cultural difference and the incredible mixture of towering modern architecture and ancient customs and ways.

Arrival at Hong Kong confirmed that this was a wealthy city. My travels have taken me to many airports, but nothing compared to the magnificence of Hong Kong's modern air terminal. Vast and remarkably airy, this huge tent-like building is remarkably relaxing.

I took the airport bus into the city and gasped at the density of the buildings. They climbed skywards – lofty narrow cubes of steel, aluminium and glass. Some, still under construction, were draped in scaffolding. Not the steel scaffolding with which we are familiar, but length after length of bamboo, lashed together with what appeared to be hemp rope! I knew that I had arrived in a very different culture.

In this city of teeming millions some back-up was needed. What better than that of the Police Department? By good fortune, I had established contact with Rod Mason and Mark Newman of the Hong Kong Police. Mark, an exiled English bobby, is Chief Inspector of Aberdeen Division and his assistance was invaluable in arranging escorts and guides to the wonders of this amazing metropolis.

I was told that the finest view of Aberdeen is from the heights of The Peak, a hill which stands above the city. To get there, I took the Peak Tramway and discovered the contribution of an Aberdonian! On 20 May, 1881, a petition was presented to Sir John Pope Hennessy, Governor of Hong Kong, on behalf of Alexander Findlay Smith, formerly of the Highland Railway Company, Scotland. This petition sought permission to build the Peak Tramway which would connect Aberdeen Harbour to the top of the Peak, some twelve to eighteen hundred feet above the city.

The work began in 1885 and the tramway was operating by 1888. The

The Aerial Tramway climbs to the Peak of Hong Kong

Aberdeen Harbour's new walkway

A local 'fishing-folks' festival

Alan contemplates his next shot

'Enter the Dragon'

Skyscrapers shelter Aberdeen Harbour

new Hong Kong Tramway was the first such engineering project in all of Asia, and its construction lay in very capable hands – Scottish, of course! The Consulting Engineer was W. Smith C.E. of Glasgow University and the Resident Engineer was James Fettes Boulton, Associate M.I.C.E., from Aberdeen, who had left his native city in Scotland to build an aerial tramway in a very distant Aberdeen.

Denis Scott, a friend back home, has one of the special silk bound commemorative books which were produced for the Tramway opening in April 1888. It claims that:

Those who know Hong Kong with its hitherto almost entire absence of suburban advantages for its rapidly increasing population, will understand the immense boom this Railway has conferred on many, who are now enabled to have detached villas and terraces on the healthy southern slopes, and on others who can leave the sun baked, stifling atmosphere of the city and in ten minutes enjoy the pure, cool breezes of the mountain tops.

A living tribute to Scottish engineering.

From the Peak, I looked down over the city and could make out the inlet where Aberdeen lay. It was time to explore it! George, a local Police Inspector, walked round the ancient fishing harbour with me, naming the various catches which had been landed that morning. The names of the fish were unfamiliar, however, I recall seeing shark, blowfish, conger eel, the poisonous stone fish, crab, oysters, mussels, and tank after tank of exotic marine life. This was like not like the fish market I visited in my childhood back home in Scotland!

The landed fish are kept in tanks of salt water, because the Chinese prefer their fish to be delivered to shops and restaurants alive and totally fresh. All around, market workers were shelling prawns, washing oysters and loading trucks with tanks of fish, the water sloshing about at our feet. On the water, small boats called 'chugga chuggas' ferried produce to and fro, while, at a special quay, ramps led down to ferries which took visitors out to the world-famous Jumbo Floating Garden Restaurant.

Aberdeen is no longer an ancient harbour covered with floating junks, as I had seen in photographs. It is now a well organised fishing market with

Early morning Hong Kong begins to stir

an elegant quayside and a walkway which leads to other parts of the city. The streets have fine shops and the ubiquitous towering skyscrapers. However the past is not far away.

Tucked at the base of one of the highest buildings I saw a small, round, red kiln, which was throwing out a plume of white smoke. George explained that this was a 'street temple' and that passers-by stopped here to share their anxieties with a spiritual advisor. After the appropriate prayers, the troubles were written on paper, the paper thrown into the kiln and the problems would go up in smoke – visible evidence that Hong Kong has a peculiar mix of very ancient religions and cutting edge technology happily living alongside each other.

Next morning a Dragon Festival filled the streets of downtown Aberdeen. The official fishing season was about to start and the fishermen sought some divine protection. My own divine protection came in the form of Shirley Wong, an officer in Aberdeen Police Division, who guided me through the narrow streets of the older part of Aberdeen. This spectacle was not laid on for the tourists. On the contrary, this centuries old tradition was for the Chinese people of Aberdeen, specifically for those who went to sea. Local fishermen, their families and hundreds of captivated on-lookers crowded the streets in eager anticipation.

To a riotous welcome, a colourful procession of musicians led the dragons down the street, their drums, gongs and loud music heralding the arrival of sea gods and goddesses. Then the central dragon appeared, a long snaking creature with a massive head, the features exaggerated and distorted. As it spun and leapt its way through the streets, it occasionally paused in order that families could dangle cabbages and lettuces from fishing rods suspended from the balconies of the houses. The dragon gobbled these up and then spat them out. It was an incredible show of pure theatre.

The symbolism of much of it evaded me, but I was captivated by the sincerity of it all. The crowd was enthralled, urging the dragon to dance even more feverishly. In a frenzy of leaps and spins the dragon consumed some alcohol and fell to the ground, exhausted and somewhat defeated.

In this ancient tradition there lies a stern message to the fishermen. I am sure it advised them to look after themselves, eat their greens and deny the temptations of alcohol, thus ensuring safety and an abundant catch. Without doubt, I had witnessed a moving event, which had genuine

Hong Kong sketch

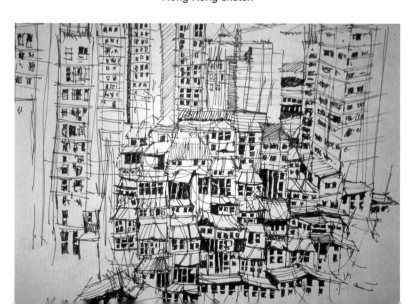

The 98 for Aberdeen — but which one!

meaning to the fishing folk of this Aberdeen. Hong Kong was proving to be a quite remarkable experience and I had a fleeting moment of confusion when a bus passed by with 'Aberdeen' written in English and Chinese on its indicator board.

'That has a long way to go!' I thought.

After the festival, a look at Hong Kong night-life was an essential experience. To be in Hong Kong after dark is to be like a startled rabbit, caught in the headlamps of some exotic vehicle. As the office blocks and hi-rise flats spill people out on to the streets, there is barely room to turn sideways. Flashing advertising signs and neon garlands of flowers illuminate this wonderland. They speak not of the city, but of a celebration of success. It was as if the Dragon Festival was merely an overture to the full evening performance!

However, it was my final evening in the city and the Hong Kong Police decided that I should have a grand gourmet farewell. A proper Chinese meal was essential. The revolving platter on the table offered a choice of beef, pork, seafood, chicken and other delicacies, prepared in a way which bore no relationship to Chinese meals back home. Each dish possessed a unique flavour, texture and aroma. All were sampled and all were exquisite!

Outside, the city and its riot of colour swept along like a crazy rainbow, providing me with powerful visual memories of my few days spent there. Here on the southern coast of this vast country is a magnificent example of the successful marriage of the truly ancient and the truly remarkable. The name Aberdeen is here, a name from distant Scotland, where our culture deals with the human spirit in a less expressive manner.

Perhaps we have something to learn. Somehow, however, I cannot see the folks of Fittie agreeing to a Dragon Festival. I must have a word with the City Council when I get home.

ABERDEEN, ANDAMAN ISLANDS

A Jail, Haddo Docks and a Bazaar

South Andaman Island lies in the Indian Ocean, in the Bay of Bengal. Here, an Aberdeen lies in the very centre of the capital Port Blair.

The long flight with overnight stops at Bombay and Madras introduced me to the cultural splendour of India. On a magical evening I ate curried fish on a rooftop high above Madras. Beneath, the city generated a symphony of noise and activity, which rose and fell as all good compositions should. The purple sky provided a backdrop to the city illuminations, reflecting red, gold and a myriad of flashing lights as all below celebrated 'night life'.

Next morning, after a one thousand mile flight across the Indian Ocean, South Andaman Island emerged from the rising mist below. Arrival at the small airport dispelled all such thoughts of relaxing after my journey, as an elegant bearded figure glided past me on wooden sandals. A magnificent orange silk robe encircled his waist and was draped over his shoulders. The same colour of silk was wound round his abundant hair, forming a tall chef-like hat. This was a 'swami', a highly respected teacher of Hindu, on a visit to South Andaman. There is so much to see in Asia. The luxury of an eye blink might deny me the unique sights of this continent.

Groves of massive palms encircled the airfield, water buffalo wandered the surrounding roads and the hot, moist air hummed with insect life. Could there possibly be an Aberdeen, here in the Bay of Bengal?

Enquiring about the possibility of accommodation, I fell on my luck when I met Kirti Singh at the desk of the Tourism Board in the small airport. Kirti was excited about someone from Scotland coming to visit her own Aberdeen. She proved to be a most valuable contact and immediately arranged a driver to take me to the Megapode Nest. This guest house, named after the tropical bird, sits on a hill-top overlooking the sparkling

Scottish thrift reaches the Bay of Bengal

waters of the Bay of Bengal. It had been a colonial bungalow with a large central building and beyond the grassed courtyard was a separate block of adjoining guest rooms. My guess that this may have been Officer's Quarters during British Empire occupation was confirmed on unlocking the large brass padlock on my room door. Clearly stamped on the lock was 'Made in Birmingham'.

A vision of British Army Officers serving in India and living here was forming quite clearly in my mind. I could hear their curt, clipped accents and the 'chink' of teacups as I sat at a table with a cool drink, gazing across the palm trees to a shimmering ocean sprinkled with tiny islands. The past could be sensed in this place. I was touching upon the history of South Andaman Island and, thanks to Kirti and her uncle Mr Baghat Singh, much more of the island's past was later to be revealed.

I was fortunate to be here, for more than one reason. The island has a restricted number of visitors and I had waited many months for an appropriate visitor's visa, allocating five days only. There is a reason for India protecting this chain of islands. Restrictions are imposed to limit casual visitors to outlying islands where people live as they did centuries ago. The Jarawas, Onges, Sentinelese, Shompens and Nicobarese still attract some of the world's leading anthropologists. These aboriginal groups are very vulnerable to the influence and illnesses of outsiders, and the Indian Government shows great wisdom in protecting these people.

South Andaman is but one of a chain of over 570 islands north of Java and Sumatra. The islands produce spices, papaya, cashew, lemon, orange, watermelon, banana, and countless other tropical fruits. The Andamans are grouped as one with the Nicobar Islands – the legendary Spice Islands. They were a mystery to Europe until the East India Company started to show an interest in them.

Lord Cornwallis, Governor General of India, wanted to establish a British colony on the islands and this was achieved in 1788. Lt. Archibald Blair reached the Andamans in 1789 and many years later, in recognition of his services, the capital was named Port Blair.

Port Blair is where the Aberdeen which I was seeking can be found. It is the commercial heart of the capital. To study the history of this fascinating island is to study the turbulent story of India's brave struggle for independence from colonial rule.

An ideal haven for the British Navy, South Andaman also provided an ideal location for a proposed penal colony: remote and one thousand miles from the east coast of mainland India. The revolt of 1857 provided the incentive to proceed with building a jail and this was constructed by 1867.

A sombre walk past the cells in the Cellular Jail

Typical Andaman corner shop

An unforgettable tropical island

Dense jungle just beyond town

Downtown Aberdeen, South Andaman Island

Net-mending Andaman fishermen

Most of the prisoners were well-to-do members of Indian society – Zaminders and Nawabs. Many were writers and poets; the usual group whose free thinking is crushed.

In a brave attempt to resist occupation the local people, who may have been Malay or Asian in origin, attacked Aberdeen Police Station. The poorly equipped force lost heavily, their courage recalled splendidly by a memorial to the Battle of Aberdeen on 14 May, 1859.

The reaction of the British to such local resistance was the abandonment of the old prison and the construction of a new and more fearsome one – the Cellular Jail. This Bastille of India was completed in 1906 in the design of a lotus leaf. It had 698 cells. Numerous political prisoners were held here and of those who were not executed, many died or committed suicide, such were the dreadful conditions at the jail.

When I finally met with Mr Baghat Singh (a most learned historian and resident of Port Blair), I heard of the long years of suffering which were endured by the unfortunate souls incarcerated in such an appalling place. Later, I visited this chilling and grim memorial to the past.

A vast building, the Cellular Jail is well named. A long, two-storey wall faced me and, on each level, row upon row of cells. The cells are small and capable of housing three or four inmates. In its time there might have been twenty or thirty prisoners crammed into these dark and suffocating holes.

In the courtyard, the place of execution made me wince, as I attempted to distance myself from association with the British Empire. Mr Singh spoke with fierce pride of generations of freedom fighters. They gave their lives in the fight against occupation.

Finally, in World War Two, the British fled the island, only to leave it to fall into the hands of the Japanese, who occupied the island for some years. Again, the people of South Andaman endured harsh and cruel treatment, and the island has many memorials recording the atrocities which were inflicted on the Andamanese.

However, these years have passed into history and, while we must reflect, we must move on as South Andaman has done. It welcomes all visitors and I met with many charming and courteous people.

I was still seeking an explanation for how the name Aberdeen had reached the Bay of Bengal, and I thought that I knew of a possible trading connection to these remote islands. For generations, creels and other fishing baskets were woven in cane by Hasties, on Commercial Quay, Aberdeen, Scotland. The cane was brought from Sumatra and Java, both of which lie to the south of the Andaman Islands. As a child I was entranced, watching the skills of the weavers as they split the cane which had been soaking in large tubs for many days. The intricate inter-twining of the cane around a woven framework swiftly became immensely strong baskets of all shapes and sizes. Could it be that merchants from north-east Scotland had used South Andaman as a trading base?

With this possible explanation in mind, I set off round the island to capture more of this exotic place. The driver took time to show me the impenetrable tropical jungle beyond the acres of rice fields. It was quite astonishing, with bamboo reaching more than thirty feet in height. Could this be where the scaffolding is grown for Hong Kong?

In the late afternoon, we arrived at the harbour, which led to further surprise and the answer to my earlier query. The harbour is called 'Haddo Docks' and was named after Haddo House, home to Lord Aberdeen in

Scotland. At last, I understood how the name Aberdeen had come to the Bay of Bengal.

Echoing around the harbour was the sound of men chipping away at wood. I could tell by the ring of the adzes and hammers that the material being worked was a hardwood. The islands have an abundant supply of padauk, kokko, marble wood, satin wood, chuglam, pongyet and many other durable native timbers. The skills which have been practised for centuries are still used by the boat builders of the Andamans.

Near the harbour, I visited one of Asia's largest sawmills and watched these dark and red woods being hauled off to the voracious teeth of the saws. Only a steamy, hot climate produces these timbers and as the day progressed it grew warmer and stickier. Yet there were still places to visit and it was time to go to the commercial centre of Port Blair and find Aberdeen itself.

What an amazing place! Aberdeen Bazaar made my eyes smile as I soaked in one visual delight after another. Painted corrugated roofs shouldered each other in sculptural friendship, sheltering stall after stall. All around, I saw the skills of local craftsmen in finely carved statues and hardwood furniture. There were hand-beaten metal bowls and containers of

Aberdeen shoppers come to town

all sizes, lengths of woven and printed fabrics, strings of painted dried nuts and semi-precious stones set in silver and gold. Exotic fruits, sacks of rice and succulent vegetables lay alongside an array of tempting home-made Asian delicacies! I was utterly enthralled. This is a creative community which does not rely on constant provision from outside factories or suppliers. If it is not available, make it yourself! The variety and quality of local craftsmanship astounded me.

Not far off, traffic encircled a roundabout, creating constant peripheral movement, and my eyes worked overtime to store all these engaging images. Under the shade of an umbrella, a lone policeman signalled energetically to the colourful buses. Rattling taxis, weaving three-wheeled canvas covered bikes and shoppers dodged the traffic. Another normal day in Aberdeen!

There is a feel of older India here, enhanced by the flowing silks of the women and young girls who seemed to glide from stall to stall, never hurried, always with elegance. I wanted to stay on, but visa-time was running out and a distant home in Scotland returned to mind. It was strange to think that many years ago, for different reasons, other Scots had walked these same streets and had looked over the same Indian Ocean. Sadly, my stay on the island and the global journey was coming to an end. A traditional Indian meal at the home of Mr Baghat Singh, in the company of his delightful family, was a fitting farewell to South Andaman Island.

Memories? Too many to recall, they come back in bursts as delightful cameos. The pieces of coral washed up on the hot sands; the incredibly dense palm forest at the National Park; water buffalo caked in dried mud; a sleeping cow in the garden of the guest house; spice-filled air; the buzz of the bazaar; and the deepest and darkest indigo night sky.

Andaman Island is a unique and fitting member of our global family.

Journey's End ?

It was time to return to Scotland and reflect on a wondrous experience. Each of the many thousands of miles imprinted powerful visual memories. The ochre landscapes of Montana and Idaho, gleaming white peaks of the High Sierra, Canada's vast orange and red prairie sunsets, the feathery white cotton fields of Mississippi, vibrant greens of the Caribbean, the attack of colour in Hong Kong and the burnished coppers of Andaman's bazaar. These are but a handful, a mere sample of countless rich recollections.

However, the most lasting memories are of warm smiles, laughter, kindness and genuine enthusiasm for our newly discovered family.

To all the Aberdeens I can only express an inadequate 'Thank you'.

A special word of appreciation is due to my travelling partner, Alan White. His was the responsibility of filming the Aberdeens and putting together my complicated journey in a visual form. His video continues to carry me back to the locations and people I had the privilege of visiting. Alan's companionship was reassuring and we *almost* kept each other out of mischief on more than one occasion! For both of us, it was a constant thrill to repeatedly see the name Aberdeen.

The 'Saltire', or St Andrew's Cross of Scotland, is Europe's oldest national flag, dating back to 832 AD. It appears on the flags of Nova Scotia, Virginia and Jamaica – proof indeed that we are and always have been, a truly international people. Now that we know of each other, I hope that the Aberdeens will move closer together. We have a history to share, and an alliance to forge. Global kinship need not be a dream.

MORE Aberdeens

ABERDEEN, WEST AFRICA

On the northern fringes of the Grain Coast of West Africa, the beautiful country of Sierra Leone has been the location of an Aberdeen since the eighteenth century. The capital, Freetown, was founded in 1787, and the name 'Aberdeen' may have originated from the captain of one of the ships which played its part in returning homeless slaves from Britain to their homeland in Africa. Since those years, when the inhabitants comprised mostly of the original Sherbros tribe and European settlers, the population of Aberdeen has grown to around 7,000.

Aberdeen now forms part of greater Freetown and is bounded on the north by Cape Light House, on the east by the River Rokel and on the south by Aberdeen Creek. The town lies about five miles from the capital city, connected by a bridge which was constructed in the 1980s.

A British colony since 1808, Sierra Leone became independent in 1961. In the 1960s, The National Dance Theatre of Sierra Leone appeared in H. M. Theatre in Aberdeen, Scotland. I can still recall the vitality, colour and movement of a magical performance.

To my regret, I never managed to visit this Aberdeen, but I do intend to, should the opportunity arise.

ABERDEEN, TASMANIA

In north Tasmania, south of the city of Devenport is an Aberdeen. It lies close to the Don River and two miles east of Melrose. The first settlers were Scots miners, arriving here in 1855. When coal stocks ran out, some turned to farming and named the district 'Aberdeen', in tribute to their heritage.

I'm sorry I didn't make it here – only having heard of it during the flight from Sydney to Los Angeles; too late to change my plans. Next time perhaps?

ABERDEEN, GUYANA

To combat the cold, Aberdeen fishermen have long appreciated the warmth of Watson's Demerara Rum. On the label of the bottle is written 'Produce of Guyana'. Many Scots worked on the sugar plantations of what used to be British Guyana, and it is very likely that someone from the north east gave the name to this small village just outside the capital city of Georgetown.

With my strong connection to a family of fishermen and my dislike of the cold, this Aberdeen is definitely on my list for a future visit!

ABERDEEN GARDENS, VIRGINIA, USA

At the edge of Hampton City, there is a suburb called Aberdeen. It is recorded in a book of letters, journals and dairy notes of the Fleet family, who have lived at 'Green Mount' plantation from 1835 to the present day.

Green Mount plantation educated the young women of the county and was a 400-acre working farm with slaves. In 1914 the grandfather of Wayne Watkins acquired a property in the area called 'Aberdeen Academy'. He bought it from the estate of J. C. Council who had been the headmaster and owner from 1859 to 1900. Aberdeen Academy was responsible for the education and military training of the young men in the county, with an average enrolment of 35 to 40 day students and around 15 boarding students.

David Fleet, who, you may recollect, named Aberdeen, Washington (see page 89), was one of the Academy's students. Further confirmation of his role in naming the new town in Washington Territory lies in his letter of 1883.

> Am going to open a Civil Engineer and Surveyor's Office in connection with the real estate business. Montesano is at the head of navigation of the Chehalis River, which empties into Gray's Harbor, some miles to the west. Two gentlemen – the proprietor of the hotel where I am staying at $6 per week, and the editor of the Vidette – have spoken to me about laying off a town down river and have promised me the selling of the lots.

A clear connection between Aberdeen Academy, Virginia, and Aberdeen, Washington.

Aberdeen, Virginia, is probably among the oldest outwith Scotland. This suburb of Hampton City was improved in the 1930s by President Roosevelt's 'New Deal', when the previous inadequate housing was replaced by superior accommodation for the black workers at the nearby US Naval Dockyards in Portsmouth. Today it is a compact district, with well laid-out, tidy gardens and a splendid local school. As for the Academy, it is now home to Wayne and Betsy Watkins and is called 'Aberdeen Farm'. Wayne has traced his roots to the Forbes Clan and Betsy was born in Dunoon, Scotland.

My visit here was all too brief.

ABERDEEN, TEXAS, USA

Rocking Chair Ranch was bought in 1889 by the Earl of Aberdeen, and was renamed 'Aberdeen'. Once boasting a blacksmith shop, hotel, store, school, post office and church, it contended for the county seat of Collingsworth Co., but the town of Wellington was chosen instead. In 1960, Aberdeen's small handful of residents moved away, and all evidence of it had gone by 1963.

There are suburbs of cities, rivers and lakes which carry the name 'Aberdeen'. An Aberdeen in Ontario, Canada, has vanished. There is a Bon Accord in Tobago. Aberdeen Park is a municipal park close to Nashville, Tennessee. In Georgia, close to Atlanta, is a golf course complex called 'Aberdeen'.

By strange coincidence, in Kamloops, British Columbia, Canada, where my brother Tom passed his last years, there is an 'Aberdeen Shopping Mall'.

And closer to Scotland . . . In the 1850s Andrew Leslie left Aberdeen, Scotland, for Tyneside, England. His arrival heralded the beginning of shipbuilding in Hebburn, just ten miles east of Newcastle upon Tyne. The many workers who followed Leslie ensured the locality became known as 'Little Aberdeen'.

Also in England there is a district within Blackrod, near Manchester, which is called Aberdeen.

My search may go on. Care to join me?

THE JOURNEY

Would I repeat such a global voyage?

Try me. When is the next flight?

The 95,438 mile journey led me to thirty Aberdeens and introduced me to fellow Aberdonians who now know that they belong to a 'global family'.

Perhaps we should be thinking about visiting each other. For all of us, there may yet be more journeys to make so that we can meet, gossip and delight in our centuries-old shared heritage.

12 – 18 OCTOBER, 2000

Fly Scotland to Amsterdam.

Fly Amsterdam to Atlanta, USA.

Drive to Aberdeen, Mississippi.

Return to Atlanta.

Fly Atlanta to Amsterdam.

Fly Amsterdam to Scotland.

22 FEBRUARY – 30 MARCH, 2001

Fly Scotland to London.

Fly London to Johannesburg, South Africa.

Fly Johannesburg to Port Elizabeth.

Drive to Aberdeen, Cape Province.

Return to Port Elizabeth.

Fly Port Elizabeth to Johannesburg.

Fly Johannesburg to Hong Kong.

Fly Hong Kong to Bombay, India.

Fly Bombay to Madras.

Fly Madras to South Andaman Island.

Fly South Andaman Island to Madras.

Fly Madras to Bombay.

Fly Bombay to Aberdeen, Hong Kong.

Fly Hong Kong to Sydney, Australia.
Drive to Aberdeen, New South Wales.
Return to Sydney.
Fly Sydney to Los Angeles, USA.
Drive to Aberdeen, California.
Drive to Reno, Nevada.
Fly to Seattle, Washington.
Drive to Aberdeen, Washington.
Return to Seattle.
Fly to Chicago, Illinois.
Fly to Newark, New Jersey.
Drive to Aberdeen, New Jersey.
Return to Newark.
Fly to Miami, Florida.
Drive to Aberdeen, Florida.
Return to Miami.
Fly Miami to Kingston, Jamaica.
Drive to Aberdeen, Jamaica.
Return to Kingston.
Fly Kingston to Miami.
Fly Miami to St Johns, Antigua.
Drive to Aberdeen, Antigua.
Return to St Johns.
Fly to Amsterdam.
Fly Amsterdam to Scotland.

5 JUNE – 6 JULY, 2001

Fly Scotland to Amsterdam.
Fly Amsterdam to Indianapolis, USA.
Drive to Aberdeen, Ohio.
Drive to Aberdeen, Indiana.
Drive to Indianapolis.
Fly Indianapolis to Parkersburg, West Virginia.
Drive to Aberdeen, West Virginia.
Drive to Aberdeen, North Carolina.
Drive to Aberdeen Gardens, Virginia.
Drive to Aberdeen, Maryland.

Drive to Aberdeen, Pennsylvania 1.
Drive to Aberdeen, Pennsylvania 2.
Drive to Scranton, Pennsylvania.
Fly Scranton to Halifax, Canada.
Drive to Aberdeen, Cape Breton 1.
Drive to Aberdeen, Cape Breton 2.
Return to Halifax.
Fly Halifax to Minneapolis, USA
Fly Minneapolis to Aberdeen, S. Dakota.
Fly to Minneapolis.
Fly Minneapolis to Billings, Montana.
Drive to Aberdeen, Montana.
Return to Billings.
Fly Billings to Minneapolis.
Fly Minneapolis to Saskatoon, Canada.
Drive to Aberdeen, Saskatchewan.
Return to Saskatoon.
Fly Saskatoon to Edmonton.
Drive Edmonton to Bon Accord, Alberta.
Return to Edmonton.
Fly Edmonton to Boise, Idaho, USA.
Drive to Aberdeen, Idaho.
Return to Boise.
Fly Boise to Amsterdam.
Fly Amsterdam to Scotland.

26 September – 2 October, 2001

Fly Scotland to Amsterdam.
Fly Amsterdam to Atlanta, USA.
Drive to Aberdeen Park, Tennessee.
Drive to Aberdeen, Kentucky.
Drive to Aberdeen, Arkansas.
Drive to Aberdeen, Mississippi.
Return to Atlanta by Aberdeen, Georgia.
Fly Atlanta to Amsterdam.
Fly Amsterdam to Scotland.

SNAPSHOTS

Journeys imprint memories. They return to me in vivid snapshots.

22 FEBRUARY

The big day of departure and I was full of anticipation at the prospect of travelling the world. The press, friends and family had said their farewells and had left the airport. Then came the information that 'Due to technical problems the flight to Heathrow will be delayed'. It seemed that we were not going anywhere. Months of planning thwarted at the first step!

More than likely, I would be spending the night in the airport only to then face the undoubted embarrassment of being seen in my Aberdeen the next day, when the local press was running an article about how I was off to the other Aberdeens!

A late flight, however, did take us to London, where we missed the connection to Johannesburg. To add to the fun, my luggage went missing.

It did not catch up with me until Hong Kong, twelve days later!

If there are hitches, better to have them at the beginning!

8 MARCH

Our friends in Hong Kong Police invited us to the Inspectors Club which sits on the waterfront. From an elegant terrace, I looked directly at the dazzling 'Jumbo Floating Restaurant'.

Office towers floodlit in green, purple, red, blue and white, created a backdrop of stunning light. Pure theatre! With eyes closed, I can still see it.

On our way back to the hotel by taxi, we suspected that the driver had 'gone round the block' more than once to bump up the fare. Alan became a ferocious Scots terrier and threatened unpredictable wrath on the driver.

The driver's understanding of spoken English dramatically improved when offered appropriate payment. It was accepted. I was impressed by my companion, as were dozens of innocent bystanders!

16 MARCH

Peter, who had been a superb host in California, drove us from Owen's Valley north to Reno, Nevada, in order that more could be seen of the stunning landscape. This was to be a long day, but, thanks to Peter's efforts, it was very memorable.

As we climbed out of Owen's Valley, we looked down on vast salt lakes and ahead to the snow-capped peaks surrounding the Mammoth Ski Resort. At the Ski Resort, the landscape positively sparkled with deep snow, beneath one of the clearest blue skies one could imagine.

Many miles beyond, we crossed a high plateau and entered Carson City. This conserved 'western town' is a time capsule from the days of Nevada's gold and silver prospecting. Striding along the wooden sidewalks, I was transported back in time as I dropped in by the original candy-shop, assay office and saloon. For a moment or two I was back in the 1880s.

But a flight to Seattle had to be met and by late afternoon we had arrived at the famous 'Gambling City' of Reno. A fond farewell to Peter and his wife Darlene and then we had to kill time in the airport, which was like no other that I had ever seen. Having a gamble at the bar was one thing, but even the public rest-rooms are filled with slot machines of all description. A 'losers' paradise!

The flight was late and on arrival at Seattle I was delighted and relieved to meet up with my relatives, Alick Lee-Warner and his son Nathan. They offered to lead us out of this vast city and on to the road which led to Aberdeen, on the coast. They did a grand job, leading us safely to the city suburbs, and then we were on our own. Whatever navigating or driving skills we had were about to be put to the test in the rainy darkness.

A full hour later, we stumbled upon the road we were seeking. It was less than half a mile from where we had parted from Alick and Nathan! At that discovery, two weary travellers exchanged a fairly heated opinion or two. Talk about 'Gormless in Seattle'!

It had been a day to remember.

24 March

Kingston Airport and a warm greeting from Addia Miller of the Jamaican Tourist Board. Because of a tiny detail on a declaration form, the Customs Officer halted our progress. We could enter Jamaica, but not with the film camera. Not without a deposit of one and a half times its value. We were talking big money, very big money. Addia came up with a solution and phoned her 'man at the top', the Minister of Tourism.

A few executive words were said to the airport officials and after almost two hours, we left the airport, camera in hand.

Thanks, Addia. Jamaica has its ways!

10 June

The drive from West Virginia to North Carolina was sensational. Through the Appalachians, over the Allegheny mountains, across the Shenandoah, on to George Washington Forest and Richmond, Virginia. In the Alleghenys we stopped at Seneca Rocks to admire the mountain scenery. It could have been Austria.

The Appalachians are magnificent. Hill after hill rolls to the horizon and the valley road snakes alongside sparkling creeks. Across these, delicate old wooden bridges lead off into dense woodland. The faint line of the distant Blue Mountains came into view as we crested yet another ridge. We stopped, compelled to soak in the landscape.

A welcome break in Richmond, then south to Raleigh, reaching Aberdeen, North Carolina after dark.

It had been a long day, but each of the six hundred miles was memorable.

15 June

To Maryland from Virginia by way of the vast Chesapeake Bridge: a monster which spans across more than eleven miles of Chesapeake Bay. Midway, we paused at the tourist centre and saw US Navy vessels heading out to sea. A truly awesome sight.

23 June

Landed at Minneapolis Airport and presented my passport at the desk. The official looked at it, noted my birthplace and studied my face.

'You are the guy visiting all the Aberdeens,' she declared, 'I have seen the article in *People Weekly*.'

Word of the journey was out!

4 July

A memorable day in Idaho. The Fourth of July was warming up in Pocatello and we stayed for the street parade. Trucks, motorcycles and a pipe band marched round the city square which was alive with local people and the Stars and Stripes. A nation celebrating!

In searing heat, we drove back to Boise from Pocatello via Craters of the Moon, Atomic City (US Dept of Energy) and Arco, where atomic energy was first exploited. Remote and fascinating places. Then on to Goodale Cut Off, a dramatic mountain pass through which Donald McKenzie forged a new route to Oregon. Standing high above the steep sides of the pass, I could scarcely believe the steely courage of those pioneers.

It was a humbling moment.

28 September

Deepest Kentucky. The hard look of the military clad guys in the store, and the back shop display of rifles, ammunition and cross-bows made me anxious. Relax, I told myself, they were here for the duck, bear or turkey. It was hunting season!

And so it went on, one memory piling on top of another. Among the many recollections were comments which still amuse and delight.

Don Gisi in South Dakota told me that the local Sioux Indians suspect that white men are lazy. He said that they refer to cycling as 'walking, sitting down'.

Jim Dorrell, who needs
to know the time in Indiana

In Indiana, Jim Dorrell arranged to meet a friend in town. They agreed 2pm. 'Will that be new time or old time?' asked Jim. Living on the line between two time zones can be confusing.

In Aberdeen, Saskatchewan, I was followed all day by TV reporter Sophia. Despite lugging a heavy-duty camera and tripod from morning to late evening, she said with warmth and a hint of a tear in her eyes, 'This is bringing us all closer together.'

In New South Wales, a sweet old lady touched my arm and asked, 'Do you know the words of the second verse of *My Granny's Heilan' Hame*? My mother used to sing it to me when I was a child, but she always burst into tears before the second verse.'

And the most amusing and valued confirmation of my many years of hard work was when I was approached by a passer-by in Aberdeen, Kentucky, and asked where I had come from and why I was in town. When I explained my research and journey, he paused, sniffed, squinted at me in disbelief, then replied in a slow drawl,

'You mean there's another Aberdeen?'

ACKNOWLEDGEMENTS

USA

Caroline Green, New Jersey
Ed Fitzgerald, New Jersey
Mark Coren, New Jersey
Brian Dougherty, New Jersey
Joel Mack, New Jersey
Clark Cox, North Carolina
Tony Robertson, North Carolina
Martha Swaringen, North Carolina
Ruth Duguid, Maryland
Peter Dacey, Maryland
Darlene Ostroski, Maryland
Charlotte Cronin, Maryland
Susan Evans, Mississippi
Clyde Wilson, Mississippi
Donald Forbes, Florida
Peter & Darlene Korngiebel, California
Marty & Diane Fortney, California
Jim Saylor, California
Kay A. Haag, Ohio
John R Mitchell, Ohio
Seth Hervey, Arkansas
Edna West, Arkansas
Dillon Dorrell, Indiana
Andrea Myler, Idaho
Mrs Wryde, Idaho
Alan Millar, Pennsylvania
Art Buntin, South Dakota
Brenda Moore, South Dakota
Carolyn Hall, West Virginia
Carolyn Washington, Virginia
Wayne & Betsy Watkins, Virginia
Angela Endres, Washington
Bill Jones, Washington
Al Waters, Washington

CANADA

Malcolm & Ingrid Weir, Saskatchewan
Ed & Marlene Decker, Saskatchewan
Brenda Tryhuba, Saskatchewan
Bea Huffman, Saskatchewan
Allan Matheson, Cape Breton
Dave & Ann Latta, Alberta

REPUBLIC OF SOUTH AFRICA

David Cresswell, Rep. of S. Africa
Eric & Joyce North, Rep. of S. Africa
Jean & John Watermeyer, Rep. of S. Africa

SIERRA LEONE

Kona F. Seibure, Sierra Leone

PEOPLES REPUBLIC OF CHINA

Mark Newman, Hong Kong
Rod Mason, Hong Kong

ANDAMAN & NICOBAR ISLANDS

Mr Baghat Singh, S. Andaman Island
Ms Kirti Singh, S. Andaman Island

CARIBBEAN

Lorraine Taylor, Jamaica
Wallace Thomson, Jamaica
Yvonne Daley, Jamaica
Claudette Rose, Jamaica
Patricia Joseph, Antigua

AUSTRALIA

Val Snow, New South Wales
Les Parsons, New South Wales
Charles Scarafiotti, Tasmania

SCOTLAND

Marcus Bowman & Kenny Murray, Ayr
Brian Daniels, Prestwick
Brian Woodcock, Aberdeen
Dennis Scott, Aberdeen
Dr John Bevan, Aberdeen
David Ritchie, Aberdeen
Iain Wolstenholme, Aberdeen

PHOTOGRAPHS

Aberdeen Neighbourhood Group,
    N. S. Wales
Aberdeen–Huntington Museum, Ohio
Aberdeen Historical Society,
    Saskatchewan
Malcolm Blue Historical Society,
    N. Carolina
Historical Society of Harford,
    Co. Maryland
Community Printing and Publishing,
    California
Aberdeen Journals Ltd, Scotland
Frederick Bull, Logie Coldstone, Scotland
Alan White, Collieston, Scotland
Jones Photo Co. Aberdeen, Washington
Aberdeen and Grampian Tourist Board,
    Scotland
Ray Gibson & Norman Adams, Aberdeen
    City Council, Publicity & Promotions
    Dept, Scotland

RESOURCE INFO. & ASSISTANCE

The Mitchell Library, Glasgow
The Central Library, Aberdeen
University of Paisley, Craigie Campus,
    Ayr
Aberdeen City Council, Scotland
British Airways Travel Shop, Aberdeen
Brown Co. Landmarks Commission, S.
    Dakota
Community Printing and Publishing,
    California
Bishop Museum and Historical Soc.,
    California
Aberdeen Visitors Bureau, South Dakota
Dacotah Prairie Museum, South Dakota
Mayor & Town Council, Bon Accord,
    Alberta
Aberdeen Seniors Club, Saskatchewan
Dept. of Tourism, Aberdeen, N. Carolina
Government Information Services, Hong
    Kong
Hong Kong Tourist Association, London
Gray's Harbor Chamber of Commerce,
    Washington
Evans Memorial Library, Aberdeen,
    Mississippi
Aberdeen Visitors Bureau, Mississippi
Public Library, Morgantown, Kentucky
Nova Scotia Department of Tourism,
    Halifax
The Charles Murray Memorial Fund
The Clan Forbes Society, Virginia
Township Council, Aberdeen, New Jersey
New Jersey Comm. and Econ. Growth
    Commission
Matawan-Aberdeen Chamber of
    Commerce
The National Tourism Board of Jamaica
National Tourism Board of Antigua &
    Barbuda
The Tourism Board of South Andaman
    Island

. . . and many others from whom I learned so much.

BIBLIOGRAPHY

Aberdeen, Saskatchewan (Aberdeen Historical Society), 1982

The Aberdeen Whisper (Neighbourhood Publications), N.S.W., 1997

The Album, Times and Tales of Inyo-Mono (Chalfont Press), California, 1990

Artz, Don, *The Town in the Frog Pond* (Memories Inc.), S. Dakota, 1991

Artz, Don, *The Life and Times of Dacotah Prairie Museum* (Aberdeen/Brown Co. Landmark Community), 2000

Brogden, W. A., *Aberdeen: An Architectural Guide* (The Rutland Press), 1986

Caliri, David, *Pine and Thistle* (Bethesda Presbyterian Church), 1989

Chubb and Milligan, *Leaves of Yesteryear* (Bon Accord FWUA), Alberta, 1977

The Gleaner (The Gleaner Co. Ltd), Kingston, Jamaica, 1997

Gold, W. Chalfant, *Guns and Ghost Towns* (Chalfant Press), California, 1975

Harford Historical Bulletin (The Historical Society of Harford County), 1995

History of Aberdeen, North Carolina (The Malcolm Blue Historical Society), 1976

Hopkins, Sarah, *Life Among the Piutes* (Sierra Media Inc.), 1969

Johnson, Russ and Anne, *The Ghost Town of Bodie* (Sierra Media Inc.), 1998

Kane, Sharyn and Richard Keeton, *Fiery Dawn* (US Army Publications), Ft. Bragg, 1999

Keith, Alexander, *A Thousand Years of Aberdeen* (Aberdeen University Press), Scotland, 1972

Kelley, J.F. and Don Artz, *The Railroad Hub of the Dakotas* (Commercial Club of Aberdeen), S. Dakota, 1907

Livezey, Jon, *Aberdeen, Maryland Centennial Almanac* (Council Publication), 1992

McClure, Eddie and Iwin Hansen, *Aberdeen School District, Idaho*, Aberdeen, Idaho, 1989

Murray, Charles, *The Last Poems* (Aberdeen University Press), Scotland, 1961

The Peak Tramway, A Commemorative Edition (Hong Kong Peak Tramway Company), 1888

Phaley, Hemlata, *Andaman and Nicobar Islands* (Nitin Tapas), 1996

Pomfret, John E., *The Rebellious Proprietary* (Princeton University Press), 1962

The Sampler (Aberdeen-Huntington Township Museum), Ohio, 1997

A School History of Aberdeenshire (Aberdeen County Education Committee), Scotland, 1961

Tinkler, Estelle D., *A History of Rocking Chair Ranch*, Panhandle-Plains Historical Review 15, 1942

Weston, David and Rhonda, *Blood, Sweat and Years* (Hunter Valley Printing Co.), 1992

The Wild West (Channel 4 Publications), London, 1995

Wood, Richard Coke, *The Owen's Valley and L.A. Water Controversy* (University of the Pacific), 1973

Wrinn and Lewis, *The Road of Personal Service* (Aberdeen and Rockfish Railroad), 1992

. . . and various cuttings from publications offered to me by generous Aberdonians, world wide.